The Boston Terrier

Tracy Libby

The Boston Terrier

Project Team
Editor: Dominique De Vito
Copy Editor: Carl Schutt
Design: Lundquist Design
Series Design: Mada Design
Series Originator: Dominique De Vito

T.F.H. Publications
President/CEO: Glen S. Axelrod
Executive Vice President: Mark E. Johnson
Publisher: Christopher T. Reggio
Production Manager: Kathy Bontz

T.F.H. Publications, Inc.
One TFH Plaza
Third and Union Avenues
Neptune City, NJ 07753

Printed and Bound in China
08 09 10 11 12   7 9 8 6

ISBN13 978 -0-7938-3629-1

Library of Congress Cataloging-in-Publication Data
Libby, Tracy, 1958-
The Boston terrier / Tracy Libby.
p. cm.
Includes index.
ISBN 0-7938-3629-8 (alk. paper)
1. Boston terrier. I. Title.
SF429.B7L53 2005
636.72—dc22
2005009953

This book has been published with the intent to provide accurate and authoritative information in regard to the subject matter within. While every reasonable precaution has been taken in preparation of this book, the author and publisher expressly disclaim responsibility for any errors, omissions, or adverse effects arising from the use or application of the information contained herein. The techniques and suggestions are used at the reader's discretion and are not to be considered a substitute for veterinary care. If you suspect a medical problem consult your veterinarian.

The leader in responsible animal care for over 50 years!®
www.tfh.com

TABLE OF CONTENTS

Chapter 1

History of the Boston Terrier 4
The First Bostons • Defined by Their Jobs • Direct Descendants • Modern-Day Bostons •
A Boston By Any Other Name • The BTCA Is Formed • Kennel Clubs & Registries

Chapter 2

Characteristics of the Boston Terrier 13
Studying the Standard • General Appearance • Characteristics of the Boston Terrier •
Bostons and the City • Bostons and Children • Exercise

Chapter 3

Preparing for Your Boston Terrier 31
Puppy or Adult? • Male or Female? • Where to Find Your Dog • The Pedigree • The
Registration Application • Health Records • Bill of Sale • Preparing Your Home • Doggy
Essentials • Pet Sitting, Doggie Daycare, and Boarding • Traveling With Your Boston

Chapter 4

Feeding Your Boston Terrier 55
The Basics • Homemade Diets • Bones & Raw Food Diet • Commercial Diets • Feeding
Puppies • Feeding an Adult • Supplementing the Diet • Problems with Feeding & Eating
• Is My Boston Overweight?

Chapter 5

Grooming Your Boston Terrier 79
Getting Your Boston Used to Grooming • Regular Grooming Care • Brushing • Nail
Trimming • Ear Care • Eye Care • Bathing Your Boston • Dental Care • Chew Toys for
Dental Hygiene

Chapter 6

Training and Behavior of Your Boston Terrier 95
Types of Training • Keep It Fun • Finding a Trainer • Basic Training • Crate Training •
Socialization • Disciplining Your Boston • Problem Behaviors • Problem Prevention • The
Importance of Chew Toys

Chapter 7

Advanced Training and Activities with Your Boston Terrier 133
Canine Good Citizen • Formal Obedience • Rally Obedience • Agility • Tracking •
Conformation Events (Dog Shows) • Other Fun Sports • Assistance or Service Dogs •
Therapy Dogs

Chapter 8

Health of Your Boston Terrier 149
Choosing a Veterinarian • Preventive Care For Your Boston • Common Health Concerns
for Bostons • Protecting Against Heat • Viral and Bacterial Diseases • Protozoal Intestinal
Infections • Worms (Internal Parasites) • External Parasites • Problems Specific to the
Brachycephalic Dog • Breeding Boston Terriers
The Senior Boston • Saying Goodbye

Resources and Organizations 183

Index 185

HISTORY
OF THE BOSTON TERRIER

They say truth is stranger than fiction, and nowhere does the old adage ring more true than with the history of the Boston Terrier. After all, who would have ever imagined a *mongrel* imported from England in the mid-1800s would one day evolve into the most popular breed in America? And you can't get more American than the Boston Terrier. Named after his city of origin—Boston, Massachusetts—the American Gentleman, as he is affectionately nicknamed, is a man-made breed and is as American as apple pie, baseball, and Boston baked beans. Perhaps that is why the big little dog from the illustrious city is the most irresistible of all the Boston delights.

THE FIRST BOSTONS

Boston Terrier owners are a lucky lot because the history and origin of the breed they adore is well documented. That is not the case with all breeds. In fact, the history of many breeds is shrouded in mystery, and owners and historians must rely on what has been passed down—mostly through legends and by word of mouth—from stablemen and horsemen who had the opportunity to know the breed long before our time.

Fortunately for the Boston Terrier, the majority of the breed's history is well documented, and the beginning of these dapper little dogs with their tuxedo coats can be traced to 1865—a time of civil war, religious controversy, women's suffrage, and the assassination of President Lincoln. Despite the turbulent era, it was also a time when many fine dogs imported by wealthy people began to find their way to the United States from England and Europe.

In 1865, Robert C. Hooper, a resident of Boston, Massachusetts, purchased a dog from fellow Bostonian William O'Brien. The dog imported from England was a cross between an English Bulldog and the now-extinct white English Terrier. Today, a pure-bred Boston Terrier is likely to carry the name of the breeder's kennel. However, 140 years ago it was not uncommon for a dog to take on his master's name. As a result, the mixed breed dog, with his dark brindle color and white blaze, became known as Hooper's Judge. At that time, the Boston Terrier breed did not yet exist, and it is highly unlikely Mr. Hooper ever imagined that his Judge would become the ancestor of almost all true modern Boston Terriers.

DEFINED BY THEIR JOBS

During this time, dogs were bred for a specific purpose, such as hunting, herding, guarding, and so forth. In England, the use of dogs for fighting and bull baiting was also becoming a popular pastime. Originally, the purpose of the bull breeds was to assist butchers in controlling the savage bulls that would eventually find their way to the supper table.

Before long, however, owners of bull breeds were eager to see which of their dogs was the most ferocious and capable of bringing a bull to the ground. They were a competitive lot, and thus the sport of bull baiting was born. Bulls were tethered to a wall and a dog—usually a Bulldog or bull-and-terrier cross—was sent into the pit to pin the bull by latching onto the bull's nose and lips with a vice-like grip.

The sport, which nowadays is considered to be barbaric and inhumane, required a dog that possessed strength, courage, determination, and tenacity. While the Bulldog possessed these characteristics, he provided little in the way of excitement or entertainment for the devoted and enthusiastic spectators. In order to satisfy and indulge the eager spectators, breeders of bull-baiting dogs began breeding their Bulldogs to the more athletic and agile terrier breeds. Their goal was to produce a bull-baiting dog that was scrappy and full of fighting spirit, yet smaller and more athletic than the cumbersome Bulldog. They succeeded, and the breedings produced a dog that possessed both the strength and tenacity of the Bulldog and the speed and trigger-quick reactions of the terrier. The resulting dogs became known as the bull-and-terrier crosses. When bull baiting was abolished in 1835, dog fighting, though equally illegal, began to flourish, and the new bull-and-terrier crossbreeds became the top dogs of the sport.

DIRECT DESCENDANTS

So what does all of this have to do with your gentle and charming Boston Terrier? Many historians believe Hooper's Judge, the progenitor of the Boston Terrier breed, was originally imported for the specific intention of fighting. However, Mother Nature had a plan of her own. Hooper's Judge was bred to a white bitch (female) of unknown breeding named Burnett's Gyp (also known as Burnett's Kate), who was owned by Edward Burnett of nearby Southboro, Massachusetts. This mating produced a puppy by the name of Well's Eph. Like so many dogs of that generation, little is known of Eph other than that he was bred to Tobin's Kate, a small bitch weighing about 20 pounds, golden brindle in color, and of unknown pedigree.

The litter was whelped in 1877 and produced Barnard's Tom and Atkinson's Toby. The two brothers became important foundation sires for the Boston Terrier breed and are said to have established the Boston Terrier breed type—the individual characteristics that constitute the essence of the breed—for that time period. It was a breed type that is much different than that of the Boston Terriers we know and love today.

Tom weighed about 22 pounds and had a dark brindle coat with a white blaze, collar, chest, and feet, and more closely resembled the Pit Bull or Staffordshire Terrier–type dogs than the dogs we know as today's Boston Terrier. Tom also had the typical short screw tail common in today's Boston Terriers. Legend has it that Tom's owner, J.P. Barnard, was horrified at the sight of the screw tail and carted the puppy to the veterinarian's requesting "the tail be put in splints in an effort to straighten it out." The veterinarian's reply was, "It cannot be done," and, as legends go, so started the enthusiasm for the kink in the Boston Terrier's tail. As with most legends, this story may be apocryphal. However, until further research reveals something vastly different, we can enjoy the unsubstantiated story for its anecdotal humor.

Ch. Hagerty King, a Boston Terrier whelped (born) in 1916.

MODERN-DAY BOSTONS

This is where Mother Nature intervened and set the course of the Boston Terrier breed. Whether by accident, genetic quirk, or simply fate, the offspring of these dogs possessed temperaments that were sweet, loving, gentle, and compatible—not the requisite qualities of a fighting dog. Indeed, the Boston Terrier came to be known as the American Gentleman due to its wonderful disposition! While these dogs were spirited, they were not quarrelsome and were in no way the brawlers of their ancestors. The gentle, loving temperaments were not what the breeders had anticipated, and one can only imagine their disappointment.

While it was common for wealthy people to import dogs from England and Europe, it was also customary for the servants and hired help to be the primary caretakers of these imported dogs. They were the people who cared for, bred, and fell in love with the intelligent and inquisitive offspring. One by one, stablemen, barbers, tradesmen, and professional men took a liking to the expressive, charming little dogs that were part Bulldog and part terrier.

These dogs were bred, line-bred, in-bred and presumably crossed with the smaller French Bulldog, as well as several smaller dogs imported from across the Atlantic, until about 1891 when a definite look began to emerge and a distinct breed was established that was neither Bulldog nor Bull Terrier. This new breed was first known as the *Round Headed Bull and Terrier*. Some people called them *round heads*. Others called them *American Bull Terriers*. Somewhere along the way, the name *Boston Bull* was thrown into the modern day Boston Terrier lexicon. However, historians note that while the breed was originally recognized by several names, Boston Bull was never one of them.

A BOSTON BY ANY OTHER NAME

The name of the breed caused quite a controversy, as one

can imagine. Fanciers of the English Bull Terrier and the English Bulldog were not happy with the new appropriation of their names, especially for a dog that looked nothing like their own. Rumor has it that the Bulldog Club of America thought the new breed was a menace to their own respective breed, and wanted it understood that their dog was the only true Bulldog. Since the dog originated in and around the Boston area, it was suggested the name be changed to the Boston Terrier.

In every breed there are forefathers of the breed—the dyed-in-the-wool pioneers, so to speak, who venture into unknown canine territory and set the course for the future of the breed. These early forefathers—prominent breeders, judges, veterinarians, and stockmen— knew what they wanted in the Boston Terrier and began establishing a consensus on what the breed should look like. On March 31, 1891, the first meeting of the Boston Terrier Club of America was held. About 40 men interested in the *round head* breed gathered, officers were elected, and a committee formed to draw up a breed standard. Thus the Boston Terrier Club of America was born. The first standard was presented to the club in April 1891, and still bears influence on the one used by fanciers of the breed today.

THE BTCA IS FORMED

Members of the newly formed BTCA began their determined and unwavering quest for American Kennel Club recognition. At that time, the AKC was still in its infancy, having been established only a few years earlier in 1884. At first, the BTCA was rebuffed. One might say the AKC was not *bullish* on the idea because they were not convinced the Boston Terrier was an established breed in which a number of reputable fanciers were interested, and they were not convinced the Boston Terrier, which had been established for such a short time, would breed true to type. However, in February 1893—28 years after Robert Hooper purchased Judge—the Boston Terrier breed was accepted by the AKC, making it the first American breed to gain AKC recognition. At that time, the stud registry certified 75 dogs whose ancestry could be traced for three generations to be purebred. These dogs formed the nucleus from which the modern-day purebred Boston Terrier grew.

The compact size and easygoing disposition of the Boston Terrier helped propel the breed's popularity, and the big little dog from Boston quickly outgrew his hometown. In 12 short years the Boston Terrier became the most popular breed in America. The breed fluctuated between first and second in AKC-ranked registration statistics from 1905 to 1939. While its ranking slipped from the starting lineup, the breed remained in the Top 10 until 1963, and in the Top 20 until 1970. For the next 17 years, its popularity never dipped lower than 29th. In 1998, the American Gentleman reentered the Top 20, where he has remained to this day.

KENNEL CLUBS & REGISTRIES

The American Kennel Club

The American Kennel Club was formed in 1884, and the primary objectives were to register purebred dogs and maintain a Stud Book registry. Today, the AKC's primary function continues to be a registry body, as well as to sanction dog events that promote interest in and sus-

tain the process of breeding for type and function of pure-bred dogs. However, it has grown from a small, struggling organization to an enormous nonprofit corporation that sponsors more than 15,000 dog competitions each year. The AKC is a *club of clubs* with over 500 member clubs and near-ly 5,000 affiliate clubs throughout the United States.

In addition to Agility, Conformation, Herding, Junior Showmanship, Obedience, and Tracking programs, the AKC offers the Canine Good Citizen program, a certification pro-gram that is designed to reward dogs that have good man-

The Round Headed Bull and Terrier and Boston Bull were two early names considered for the Boston Terrier.

ners at home and in the community.

The AKC also publishes the monthly magazine the *AKC Gazette*, which is geared toward serious dog enthusiasts who are interested in professional advice on showing, training, and breeding purebred dogs. It also publishes the quarterly magazine *AKC Family Dog*, which is written for the busy lifestyles of companion dog owners who are interested in anything and everything from grooming techniques to solving dog behavior problems.

The Kennel Club in the U.K.

On June 28 and 29, 1859, the first organized dog show was held in the Town Hall, Newcastle-on-Tyne. By the late 1860s, many undesirable practices were taking place, and while local clubs attempted to apply some reform, they lacked not only the requisite finances but also harmony in their policies. In April 1873, a meeting of the National Dog Club Committee was called and a discussion ensued, which resulted in the founding of England's prestigious Kennel Club. The primary objectives of the Kennel Club were related to the interests of the purebred dog and the conduct of activities at shows and trials.

During the early years, the Kennel Club implemented and maintained a universal registry of purebred dogs and recognized, licensed, or sanctioned shows. The Kennel Club was also instrumental in popularizing the sport of dog showing and moving competitions from the venues of bars and public houses to fashionable locations including the Crystal Palace and the Botanical Gardens.

Today, the Kennel Club has become increasingly concerned with anti-dog legislation and actively represents the interests of responsible dog owners whether the dog is Kennel Club registered or not. It publishes the monthly magazine *Kennel Gazette*, which is geared toward people interested in the sport of purebred dogs. It also gives numerous donations to projects including canine rescue and dogs for the disabled, and supports research into canine disease.

The Canadian Kennel Club

The CKC was formed in 1888 and registered its first Boston Terrier in 1899. The CKC is the primary all-breed registry for purebred dogs in Canada. They currently recognize over 160 breeds and, like the AKC, they are a nonprofit organization devoted to the advancement of purebred dogs. The CKC sponsors programs for Conformation, Obedience, Junior Showmanship, and Tracking. They publish the monthly magazine *Dogs in Canada*.

England's Tea Party

The origins of many fine breeds can be traced to England and Europe, but not the Boston Terrier. This breed's roots are firmly planted in red, white, and blue soil, which makes the breed a true American success story. That's not to say there are no Boston Terriers in England. There are. However, it is difficult to say precisely when the first Boston Terrier was imported to England. Historians believe it was Mr. H. Smith's Brindle Beauty in 1901. England's Kennel Club statistics show that Boston Terriers were first registered in 1937. However, prior to 1937, many breeds were simply classified under "any other breed" in the Kennel Club's statistics records. Therefore, it is possible that the breed was registered as far back as 1901. Historians also believe, although it has yet to be substantiated, that the Boston Terrier made his debut on the English show bench in 1911.

The classy "American Gentleman" has been among the best-loved breeds since the early 1900s.

The United Kennel Club

The United Kennel Club is the second largest and oldest multi-breed registry in the United States. Founded in 1898, the club recognized the Boston Terrier in 1914. The UKC sponsors canine events including Agility, Conformation, Obedience, Field Tests, and Weight Pull competitions. They publish three magazines including *Bloodlines*, a monthly magazine geared toward the serious dog enthusiast.

TODAY'S BOSTON TERRIER CLUB OF AMERICA

More than 100 years after its formation, the Boston Terrier Club of America remains the AKC parent club of the Boston Terrier, and is the driving force behind the development and improvement of the Boston Terrier.

CHARACTERISTICS
OF THE BOSTON TERRIER

E very breed has a blueprint for success. It's called the breed standard, and it describes the ideal makeup of an individual breed. To the newcomer, it may seem nothing more than a cluster of strange-sounding words strung together on a piece of paper. However, it is a detailed description of the *perfect* canine specimen, describing everything from body type and temperament to coat texture and eye color.

The Boston Terrier's breed standard was written in 1891, when the forefathers of the breed had the foresight to describe and standardize the ideal Boston Terrier. The breed standard serves not only as a gauge for breeders and judges—to help them determine the ideal quality, soundness, and beauty of the Boston Terrier—but also functions as a historical document. It can teach fanciers of the breed about the origin of the Boston Terrier, where the breed has been, and where it is going. The major points of the original Boston Terrier standard, adopted more than 100 years ago, still define the breed's characteristics.

STUDYING THE STANDARD

The Boston Terrier standard is simultaneously simplistic and complicated. It is simplistic in that it describes the ideal quality, soundness, and beauty of the Boston Terrier. What could be simpler? On the other hand, it can be complicated for newcomers and even a few experienced fanciers because of its old-fashioned words and language. Originally, people who worked their dogs, usually stockmen and horsemen, wrote most of the breed standards because they had extensive knowledge of dogs and horses under working conditions. By simply looking at a dog or horse, they could say if it was good or not. Therefore, when they wrote a standard there was an implied assumption of dog knowledge. They did not, for example, need to waste time writing in a standard that a dog had four legs. They understood *balance* meant a dog whose integral parts—head, neck, body—had a harmonious outline and were all in proportion. They knew *sound* meant free of injury or an absence of lameness. There was no need to spell it out in a standard. As a result, sorting through the terminology and converting word pictures to movement involves research and effort on the part of today's fanciers.

That said, taking the time to learn and understand the breed standard will help you figure out what makes your Boston tick. It will help explain why your Boston does what he does,

A breed's written "standard" can help define its characteristics for decades.

and why and how each component of your Boston should work together harmoniously. It is worth mentioning that breed standards often differ from country to country. Sometimes the difference is seemingly insignificant, but that small difference can be enough to change a certain aspect of a Boston Terrier. As a result, Bostons can vary slightly as one travels to different countries.

In order to help you understand the AKC Boston breed standard, some important explanations and clarifications are explained in this chapter. Excerpts from the official standard are in italics and discussed in regular text.

GENERAL APPEARANCE

The Boston Terrier is a lively, highly intelligent, smooth-coated, short-headed, compactly built, short-tailed, well-balanced dog, brindle, seal, or black in color and evenly marked with white. The head is in proportion to the size of the dog and the expression indicates a high degree of intelligence.

The body is rather short and well-knit, the limbs strong and neatly turned, the tail is short and no feature is so prominent that the dog appears badly proportioned. The dog conveys an impression of determination, strength, and activity, with style of high order; carriage easy and graceful. A proportionate combination of "Color and White Markings" is a particularly distinctive feature of a representative specimen.

The General Appearance section describes the true Boston Terrier. It gives a clear, overall description of the breed, including the dog's expression, color, markings, size, and temperament. This is a snapshot, so to speak, of the Boston taken as a whole, and what he should represent both standing still and while in motion. The subsequent sections of the breed standard explain in greater detail the specifics of the Boston Terrier breed.

Size, Proportion, and Substance

Weight is divided by classes as follows: Under 15 pounds; 15 pounds and under 20 pounds; 20 pounds and not to exceed 25 pounds. The length of leg must balance with the length of body to give the Boston Terrier its striking square appearance. The Boston Terrier is a sturdy dog and must not appear to be either spindly or coarse. The bone and muscle must be in proportion as well as an enhancement to the dog's weight and structure. Fault: Blocky or chunky in appearance.

Size is really a matter of personal preference when choosing a Boston Terrier. Some owners prefer the smaller dog. Others prefer the middleweight size, and the heavier-weight dog has a long list of admirers, too. There is no minimum height requirement for a Boston Terrier. However, regardless of the dog's weight class, there must be an evenness of type. The ideal Boston Terrier is a *well-balanced* dog, and his structure should conform to the individual weight class. A small Boston, for example, should not have a head that is too big for his body, or a body too big for his head. A Boston in the heavyweight class should not have the bone better suited for a smaller dog, and vice versa. He should be *sturdy* but never *chunky*, *spindly* (fine boned), or *coarse* (lacking refinement). When viewed from the side, a Boston's body should be compact and of relatively equal height and length. This is what gives the Boston his

Determination, strength, and intelligence are all used to describe the Boston Terrier.

square appearance; an appearance that beyond doubt defines the Boston Terrier breed and ensure the dog's movements will be sound.

Head

The skull is short, flat on top, free from wrinkles, cheeks flat, brow abrupt, and the stop well defined. The eyes are wide apart, large and round and dark in color.

One might say when it comes to Boston Terriers, it's cool to be square. A Boston's head, like his overall appearance, should be strikingly square and in proportion to the size of the dog. Often referred to as a *head breed*, the head, perhaps more so than any other feature, sets the Boston apart from other breeds and strongly contributes to the dog's breed character. It is also weighted heavily with 15 points out of a possible 100 being assigned to this aspect of the dog's conformation.

A good head is the mark of quality. The Boston's head should be free from wrinkles with a well-defined *stop*—the indentation where the nose connects with the skull. The key words being *well-defined*. Each breed has different types of

The breed standard is written for both male and female Boston Terriers; it does not differentiate between the two, and both sexes should possess equal structural quality. Most judges will look for a slight refinement in the female's conformation. A female should be feminine, and a dog should be masculine.

stops, with some appearing to be grooved out or indented, but a Boston's stop should be his own. The Boston's head is measured lengthwise from the *stop* to the back or base of the skull. This length should be the same as the width of the skull at the outside edges of the ears and the outside edges of the eyes.

Equally important, a Boston should have flat cheeks. Bulging cheeks, which are considered a serious fault, throw a dog's head out of proportion and break the square effect of the head. It is considered a serious fault if a Boston shows any tongue or teeth when his mouth is closed.

Expression

The ideal Boston Terrier expression is alert and kind, indicating a high degree of intelligence. This is a most important characteristic of the breed.

Eyes

The eyes are wide apart, large and round and dark in color. The eyes are set square in the skull and the outside corners are on a line with the cheeks as viewed from the front. Disqualify: Eyes blue in color or any trace of blue.

It is frequently said that the eyes are a window into the soul. The eyes of a Boston reflect his character, and a Boston should have a fine-looking pair of eyes. They should be wide apart and round, but not too prominent. The color of the eyes

Equally important, the white (sclera) of a Boston's eye should be scarcely visible. Too much visible white makes the dog's eyes appear to turn in opposing directions, which years ago was referred to as googly-eyed. Today, they are sometimes referred to as east-west eyes. Regardless of the term, too much white distracts from the Boston's distinct and well-defined expression.

These puppies have the distinctive heads of Boston Terriers, with dark eyes set wide apart, flat cheeks, and small ears.

should always be dark—never blue. Bostons with any blue in their eyes are disqualified from showing and should not be bred. It is worth noting that the percentage of blue-eyed Bostons is very low. Blue eyes do not present a health issue or detract from a Boston's ability to be a superb companion or accomplished athlete, provided the dog has been tested and has not been diagnosed as unilaterally or bilaterally deaf.

Ears

The ears are small, carried erect, either natural or cropped to conform to the shape of the head and situated as near to the corners of the skull as possible.

Perhaps nothing is more controversial in the breed standard than the cropping of ears. It is not a practice indigenous to the Boston breed, but it is a tradition that has come under assault for many, many years. In Britain and a few other countries, the practice of cropping ears is forbidden and has been for quite a while.

When ears are cropped, they are made to stand erect as a result of the surgical removal of a section of the earflap. More often than not, it is done for cosmetic reasons. Most Bostons have naturally erect ears, unlike some breeds in which a naturally folded ear is traditionally cropped to create an erect one. In order for a Boston's ears to be cropped, they must first stand erect. Sounds like a bit of a conundrum, right? Here's the reason: As a Boston matures, the cartilage in his ears hardens and the ears naturally stand erect. If a Boston's ears do not naturally stand erect when cropped, they will be too soft and will tip over.

Cropping may improve the appearance of the Boston, but it does not "make the dog." It is the combination of components taken as a whole—his color, markings, temperament, size— that have made him a longtime American favorite.

If you go down this road, it is essential you find a veterinarian who is experienced with Boston ears and also comes with excellent references from other show people. Ear cropping is not recommended for companion Boston Terriers, or Bostons competing in events outside of the conformation ring, such as agility, obedience, and tracking.

Muzzle

The muzzle is short, square, wide, and deep and in proportion to the skull. It is free from wrinkles, shorter in length than in width or depth; not exceeding in length approximately one-third of the length of the skull. The muzzle from the stop to the end of the nose is parallel to the top of the skull. The nose is black and wide, with a well-defined line between the nostrils. Disqualify: Dudley nose.

The Boston is a brachycephalic breed, meaning the dog's muzzle is exaggeratedly shortened. The muzzle is of primary importance and is an essential characteristic of the Boston Terrier breed. It must be in proportion to the skull. Oftentimes, a muzzle will be too short or too long for the skull going with it. If the muzzle tilts downward (when viewed from the side) it is said to be down-faced. If the muzzle has a concavity to it, it is said to be dish-faced.

A Boston's nose should be black and wide with a well-defined line between the nostrils. A Dudley nose—that is, a flesh-colored nose with no black pigmentation—is a disqualification. A nose without pigmentation is more susceptible to sunburn and solar dermatitis.

Neck, Topline, and Body

The length of the neck must display an image of balance to the total dog. It is slightly arched, carrying the head gracefully, and setting neatly into the shoulders. The back is just short enough to square the body. The topline is level and the rump curves slightly to the set-on of the tail. The chest is deep with good width, ribs well sprung and carried well to the loins. The body should appear short. The tail is set-on low, short, fine, and tapering, straight or screw and must not be carried above horizontal. (Note: the preferred tail does not exceed in length more than one-quarter the distance from setting on to hock.) Disqualify: docked tail. Body Faults: gaily carried tail.

The feet are small, round, and compact, turned neither in nor out, with well-arched toes and short nails. Faults: Legs lacking in substance; splay feet.

This section of the breed standard describes the body, limbs, and gait (movement) of the Boston Terrier. Simply

The Boston's neck should contribute to his "aristocratic bearing" by being neither too short nor too long.

The tuxedo markings definitely set the Boston apart from other breeds!

put, it addresses how the structure of the body comes together so that all the parts complement each other and work harmoniously for total flexibility, efficiency, and soundness. While the head and neck are described as separate entities within the breed standard, they work together as balancing functions.

The neck is a mark of quality and is quite important in the overall design. A Boston's neck, as called for in the breed standard, should be neither too long nor too short. It should be just the right length, slightly arched and in balance with the general appearance in order to carry the dog's head gracefully, setting neatly into the shoulders.

The Boston's back should be short—just long enough to square his body—and his topline should be level. The croup curves slightly where the rump and tail join, also known as the *set on*. If a Boston's rump is higher than the overall topline or the rump slants too much, it causes the rear gait to be faulty.

A Boston's feet are often overlooked in the grand scheme of correct conformation. However, a dog's feet are critical because they support his entire body weight in a small cross-sectional area. A compact foot, which the standard calls for, provides the most strength. Feet that are round and compact are often referred to as cat feet. Splayed feet—feet that lack tightness and compactness—are a serious fault because they weaken the entire assembly and lead to early breakdown and lameness.

Coat

The coat is short, smooth, bright, and fine in texture.

Color and Markings

Brindle, seal, or black with white markings. Brindle is preferred only if all other qualities are equal. (Note: Seal Defined. Seal appears black except it has a red cast when viewed in the sun or bright light.) Disqualify: Solid black, solid brindle, or solid seal without required markings. Gray or liver colors.

Required markings: White muzzle band, white blaze between the eyes, white forechest.

Desired markings: White muzzle band, even white blaze between the eyes and over the head, white collar, white forechest, white on part or whole of foreleg and hind legs below the hocks (Note: A representative of the specimen should not be penalized for possessing Desired Markings.) A dog with preponderance of white on the head or body must possess sufficient merit otherwise to counteract its deficiencies.

The distinct tuxedo markings set the Boston apart from other breeds. The head and face markings, which are emphasized in the standard, are important in this breed, and they add to the Boston's distinct and true expression. You will notice that the standard describes *required markings* and *desired markings*. A Boston is required to have a white muzzle band, white blaze between the eyes, and white forechest. The desired markings are considered to be the perfect, or ideal, markings in a Boston. It is important to note that a Boston with a *preponderance of white on the head or body* is not a disqualification or even a fault. In order for Bostons with a preponderance of white to win in the show ring, they must also be of exceptional conformation/championship caliber in general type in order to overcome their deficiencies in markings.

Boston Terriers without the required white markings are few and far between, but in no way extinct. They still make excellent companions even though they lack the characteristic markings that make them look like they are wearing a tuxedo.

Temperament

The Boston Terrier is a friendly and lively dog. The breed has an excellent disposition and a high degree of intelligence, which makes the Boston Terrier an incomparable companion.

The Boston Terrier may have descended from the bull-and-terrier crosses, but for the last 100 years or so he has been bred strictly as a companion dog. As a result, his temperament is exceptional. A bright look in his eyes shows the Boston's intelligence. He is an adoring, energetic, fun-loving dog that routinely chooses the company of his owners over other dogs or animals, which makes him the ideal home companion. Don't be fooled by his size, however. He is 100-percent

Sociable, happy, smart, responsive— these traits all describe the charming Boston Terrier.

dog and must be treated as such, which can otherwise spell disaster for the novice owner.

Summary

The clean-cut, short-backed body of the Boston Terrier coupled with the unique characteristics of his square head and jaw, and his striking markings have resulted in a most dapper and charming American original: The Boston Terrier.

CHARACTERISTICS OF THE BOSTON TERRIER

Personality Profile

The breed standard describes the *ideal* temperament of the Boston Terrier. In the real world, Bostons can run the gamut in temperaments from the mellow characteristics of the Bulldog to the pluck and feistiness of their terrier forebearers. In the genetic lottery, Bostons can also be shy, nervous, and fearful, as well as hyperactive or dog aggressive. Most well-bred Bostons acquired from reputable breeders fall somewhere in the middle and possess the classic Boston Terrier temperament—fun-loving, affectionate, spunky, active, animated, and curious. He also seemingly has the uncanny ability to mirror our moods. If you're happy, he's happy. If you're feeling under the weather, he feels under the weather. If you grab your shoes to go for a walk, he's likely to grab his leash.

A puppy's temperament reflects that of his mother and father.

Generally speaking, the best indicator of a puppy's temperament is the disposition and activity level of the mother and father. If, for example, a puppy is a product of parents that both possess exceptional temperaments, there is a high probability that the puppy will inherit the same exceptional temperament and will show his parents' influence throughout his life. There are, of course, exceptions to the genetic lottery and some puppies, regardless of their parents' genetic contribution, grow into adult dogs with unstable temperaments. Environmental influences and conditions under which a puppy is whelped, reared, and socialized also play an important part in defining his temperament. Most knowledgeable breeders can match the personality and temperament of a particular dog with the right family.

It is important to understand that Bostons may look small, but they are big dogs on the inside. Someone once correctly said, "Boston Terriers own the ground they stand on." They are fearless and curious in nature and have no concept of their size. While most are not hyperactive, they do possess a moderate amount of energy. And, like any energetic dog, they require both physical and mental stimulation. A Boston is always up for a ride in the car, a game of tug-of-war, or snoozing on the couch with his owner. In fact, anything on the day's schedule is okay with the Boston Terrier—as long as it doesn't involve being left alone.

The flipside is that the characteristics that make him a

Their size and disposition make the Boston well-suited to urban or suburban living, with controlled temperatures.

loyal, faithful, and devoted companion also exclude him from being an agreeable backyard or kennel dog. Boston Terriers do not make good backyard dogs, nor do they tolerate being kenneled or confined for any great period of time, such as when you go on vacation or out of town. Boston Terriers are basically indoor dogs. They are not equipped to withstand extremes in temperature. Because of their short coats, they do not like, nor can they tolerate, too much cold. A Boston's general *modus operandi* is to quickly run outside and relieve himself, then dash back inside to the comfort of his warm house. On the other hand, because of their short muzzles, they pant easily and cannot tolerate too much heat.

BOSTONS AND THE CITY

Boston Terriers don't take up much space, so they can live harmoniously in a city apartment or urban setting, provided they receive adequate exercise each day. If you live in an apartment, condominium, or a house without a fenced yard, you will need to schedule regular outdoor outings—first thing in the morning, in the afternoon, and again in the evening. If your outings include a trip to a public dog park, be sure to follow designated rules and regulations.

The danger in allowing your Boston Terrier to be exposed to excessive temperatures cannot be stressed enough. The breed's short, thin coat does not protect him from cold or wet weather, and therefore he is not a suitable outdoor dog. If your Boston is accompanying you on a short, brisk winter walk, chances are he will be fine, unless temperatures drop below freezing. You may want to consider investing in a warm winter coat or sweater and a pair of booties for your Boston if you plan to have him outdoors for extended periods of time.

Bostons cannot tolerate excessively hot temperatures, either. If your Boston must remain outdoors for any length of time, you will need to provide him with plenty of fresh water, shade, and a cool spot for sleeping. You should also restrict any type of extended exercise to the cooler parts of the day.

Whether you live in the city, suburbia, or the country, you should never allow your Boston to roam at will. Unsupervised dogs may be stolen, hit by a car, poisoned, or, at the very least, develop bad habits.

BOSTONS AND CHILDREN

If you grew up with a dog or two, no doubt you recognize the valuable and lifelong lessons children can learn from canine companions. Boston Terriers give unconditional love and companionship that can build confidence in a child. They are tireless companions and often have far more energy than parents! A Boston Terrier is an excellent companion for surviving adolescence, sharing secrets, and exploring the world, but with guidance.

Generally speaking, most even-tempered Bostons do quite well in a household when they are raised with children, established guidelines are followed, and children are clearly supervised. Bostons may have descended from the feisty terrier breed, but even the most accepting Boston might not tolerate the rough-and-tumble behavior of young kids who try to smother them with affection, tug on their ears or tails, or poke little fingers in their eyes. These types of behaviors can startle, frighten, and even injure a Boston.

Parents are the key figures when it comes to teaching children how to interact safely with dogs. From day one, it is important that you teach your child some basic common courtesies just as you would with other family members. For instance, you would not allow a child to jump on a parent or sibling who is sleeping, or barge into a bathroom without knocking. The same considerations apply to the family dog, such as teaching children not to disturb a sleeping dog, or bother a dog that is eating, playing with a toy, or chewing a bone.

Equally important, infants, babies, and young children should never, ever, under any circumstances be left alone with a dog regardless of how trustworthy your Boston may be. No dog is completely predictable with children. A dog may misread the strange sounds of an infant or the unpredictable behaviors of a toddler. Young children, generally under the age of seven, do not understand the consequences of their actions. They see nothing wrong with trying to pick up a dog by his ears or by wrapping their arms around his neck. They do not understand they can seriously injure a puppy or young dog if they pick him up incorrectly or, heaven forbid, drop him.

Children who learn to tend to the needs of their dog can learn responsibility, respect, and compassion. They learn that he will need water when he's thirsty, food when he's hungry, a bath when he's dirty, and peace and quiet when he's sleeping. At what age you begin teaching these responsibilities varies depending on the individual child. There are some things you can teach a four-year-old child, but not a three-year-old. A child's individual maturity level as they get older will dictate how much responsibility you can give them in any part of life, including the responsibility of feeding and caring for a dog.

The Finer Points of Play

Play is a wonderful way for both dogs and kids to release excess energy. They run, jump, swim, and go for bike rides. Children also need to be taught what games are and are not acceptable when playing with dogs. To prevent the situation from getting out of control, parents should always monitor and control the play between dogs and kids; play should be appropriate to the size and age of the dog as well as the child; think active rather than rough--avoid games that encourage or allow a dog to use his teeth, such as *sic 'em* or *attack* or wrestling games where a dog can become overexcited and inadvertently learn to use his teeth; play shouldn't hurt. Don't allow kids to hit, kick, pinch, punch, bite, or harass a dog in the name of play.

EXERCISE

Like humans, dogs need plenty of exercise to maintain their good health. Exercise is vital for stimulating your Boston's respiratory and circulatory systems, and for building strong bones and muscles. Exercise will ward off obesity—keeping your Boston fit and lean. It nourishes and energizes a Boston's mind, keeping him active, healthy, and alert. Exercise and interactive play between a Boston and his owner can help eliminate loneliness, stress, and boredom,

Don't neglect your older Boston Terrier. A senior dog needs exercise to keep his body and systems functioning properly. The exercise, of course, will not be as strenuous as a younger dog's, but it should be regular exercise and enough to keep him active, alert, and healthy.

which are often the primary causes of unwanted behaviors including destructive chewing and barking. Exercise is a great way to give your Boston Terrier plenty of attention while building a strong human/canine relationship.

Any exercise program needs to be tailored to suit your Boston Terrier—taking into account his age, health, and overall physical condition. A puppy, for instance, will tire more quickly than an adult Boston. Therefore, a puppy will require short but multiple exercise periods spaced throughout the day. Equally important, you will need to take plenty of care with your Boston Terrier puppy. He may act tough, but his body is young and tender, and he can easily be injured when jumping, twisting, turning, or getting body slammed by a bigger dog. A healthy adult Boston may require more than a brisk walk around the block to satisfy his energy requirements. Again, much will depend on your dog's overall physical and mental health and individual energy level.

In the winter months, when it is too cold or wet to go outside, you can exercise your smaller Boston indoors. A tennis ball or stuffed toy is soft enough and fairly safe for indoor retrieve or Find it! games. An indoor game of hide-and-seek will begin instilling the come command, as well as provide physical and mental stimulation. To play, simply toss a cookie or toy down the hall or across the room. When your Boston runs to retrieve it, you run in the opposite direction and duck behind a door or chair. When he finds you, shower him with plenty of kisses and praise saying excitedly things like, "Did you find your mommy? What a clever dog!"

As with any exercise program, it is important to start slowly and gradually work your way up to higher levels. Remember, Bostons do not tolerate excessive temperatures, be they hot or cold. So it is best to confine your exercise and training to the cooler parts of the day. If you notice signs of fatigue, including heavy panting, you should allow your Boston plenty of time to rest and cool down. If your Boston is overweight, injured, or out of condition, it is prudent to consult with your veterinarian before beginning any exercise program.

Walking and playing with your Boston are essential forms of enjoyable exercise for both of you.

3 PREPARING

No doubt about it, Boston Terrier puppies are irresistible. The same cuteness that makes them ideal subjects for countless picture postcards, greeting cards, and calendars is also responsible for many an owner taking one (or two!) home on impulse. Despite their seemingly irresistible appeal and delightful personality, acquiring a Boston, or any dog, on impulse is a bad idea. A well-bred and well-cared-for Boston Terrier can live to be 10, 11, or 12 years old. That is a significant investment for owners in terms of love, time, and patience, as well as expected and unexpected expenses.

The good news is you need not go to Boston to find the perfect Boston! Finding the right Boston does, however, require time, effort, and a bit of detective work. You'll need to do your homework and check on resources, familiarize yourself with the Boston breed standard, and research breeders. You should also talk to several Boston breeders, as well as trainers, veterinarians, and other Boston owners. Read books and magazines and attend shows. If you make wise choices in the beginning, you are more assured of having a long and happy relationship with a delightful and healthy Boston Terrier.

PUPPY OR ADULT?

Unless you have your heart set on a puppy, you might want to consider the benefits of purchasing an adult Boston Terrier. When you purchase an older Boston, say one, two or three years old, what you see is what you get. An older dog's personality is already developed. With close observation, interaction, and help from a knowledgeable dog person, you should be able to determine the quality of his disposition and whether or not he will suit your personality and daily life. Is he timid? Aggressive? Bold? Sassy? Does he have ants in his pants? Is he lively? Energetic? Happy? Is he spoiled rotten? Does he try to kiss you—a typical Boston characteristic—or does he cower in the corner? Does he get along with kids? Other animals?

Adult Boston Terriers become available for a variety of reasons and most often through no fault of their own. Many breeders, for instance, have retired show dogs they are looking to place in good companion homes. Some breeders have one- or two-year-old show prospects that did not pan out because of conformation faults, but would make exceptional pets. Oftentimes,

An older Boston Terrier may be the perfect candidate to bring the joy of canine companionship into your home.

breeders are limited in the number of dogs they can keep, and they may need to cut back on dogs to make room for up-and-coming litters, new show prospects, or trainees. Occasionally, Bostons are returned to the breeder because the owner moved or is no longer able to keep the dog. Many of these dogs are well bred and have been well cared for, yet, for one reason or another, need to be placed in a good home.

That said, purchasing an adult dog is not without risk. A show dog that has been raised in a kennel situation will most likely be crate-trained, accustomed to traveling, and oblivious to the pandemonium of shows, but he may not be housetrained. He may or may not have been raised around kids, and he may or may not like kids. If there are no problems, most kids and Boston Terriers that are properly introduced and supervised will quickly develop a strong and loving relationship that will last a lifetime.

MALE OR FEMALE?

When all is said and done, choosing a male or female dog usually comes down to personal preference. Some people have a preference for males, and others just love females. Both males and females can make loving companions, and the pros and cons of either sex seem to balance each other out. If you are undecided, here are a few things to consider:

Regardless of the breed, in most instances, male dogs (and some females) will have a natural tendency to mark their territory by hiking their leg and urinating. It's a way of saying, "I was here." A Hallmark card would be nicer, but that's not the way dogs operate. They place a scent of ownership around a territory, which can include sofas, bedspreads, laundry baskets, lawn furniture, car tires, planter boxes, and the like. Some males have been known to hike their leg on other dogs, people, and even their owner.

Intact males (males that have not been neutered) are more likely than females to roam. Some intact males, despite their mode of containment, can become talented and accomplished escape artists at the slightest whiff of a female in heat.

Intact females come into heat once they have reached their sexual maturity. This usually occurs between six and ten months of age, but can vary with individual females. Most females come into season about every six or nine months for their entire lives. Each cycle lasts about 21 days, and during this time females become fertile and receptive to mating. Confinement of a female in heat is extremely important. Twenty-four-hour house arrest comes to mind. It takes only a second of miscalculated judgement, and you've got a litter of unwanted puppies.

If you are purchasing a Boston as a competition dog—one that you plan to show in the breed ring, obedience competition, agility trials, and so forth—it is important to note that a female's training and showing schedule may be interrupted while she is in season. On the other hand, males that detect a female in season become heat-seeking missiles, so to speak. Their behavior is unmistakable. They start salivating and drooling—almost hyperventilating. Their eyes glaze over. Their brains turn to mush, and it is almost impossible to get or maintain their attention for more than a nanosecond. This can be extremely frustrating and disruptive to the handler of an obedience, agility, or tracking dog.

Unless the Boston you choose is part of a planned breeding program, it is best to leave the breeding of Boston Terrier to the experts. Spaying or neutering your Boston as soon as possible will help reduce, if not prevent, a myriad of behavioral and medical problems.

Deciding on a male or female is a significant consideration if you want to show your dog.

WHERE TO FIND YOUR DOG

Breeders

Anyone can claim to be a Boston Terrier breeder. That in itself does not make the person responsible or reputable. Breeding purebred dogs is a labor of love, as well as an art and a science. Reputable breeders are educated, conscientious, and care about the welfare of their dogs and the breed. They study pedigrees, plan litters, and breed only to maintain or improve the quality of the Boston Terrier breed. They recognize that each breeding must be undertaken with great care and forethought. They know all of the distinguishing features of their dogs' bloodlines, including temperament, and physical and mental developmental patterns.

Breeders tend to have their breeding stock tested for genetic problems and diseases, and will only breed those dogs that are proven clear of problems. Reputable breeders handle their puppies regularly and affectionately and socialize them to everything the puppies are likely to encounter as adult dogs. Most breeders perform puppy aptitude tests, or some form of evaluation, in order to assess a puppy's training requirements, competitive potential, and placement options.

They can answer questions regarding the training, grooming, feeding, handling, and showing of Boston Terriers, and dogs in general. They only sell their dogs to people who have passed screening questions and, in their opinion, meet the qualifications necessary to provide a permanent, first-class home for their Bostons. If for some reason your particular Boston Terrier does not work, a reputable breeder is often in a position to either take back the dog, help place it, or offer an appropriate solution.

It is important to keep in mind that some of the breeders you will be talking to are biased in their opinions. Of course they will tell you their puppies are the best! It is helpful to visit several breeders so you have something to compare before making your choice.

Not all who call themselves breeders are working for the betterment of Boston Terriers. There are those who breed dogs with little regard or concern for their dogs' ancestral background or the finer points of the Boston Terrier breed. They are not necessarily bad people, and they do not always have bad intentions. Some of them truly love their dogs and provide good care. However, most are unaware of the pet

All puppies are irresistible! Ask a lot of questions before choosing the one who's best for you.

overpopulation problem and don't realize they are part of the problem.

These "backyard breeders" seldom have knowledge of pedigrees, genetic disorders, or the importance of socializing puppies. Normally, they are not involved in the sport of dogs, nor do they invest the time, money, or energy into producing dogs of sound health and temperament. They are not likely to test their breeding stock or puppies for genetic diseases. Their breeding stock is generally not breed quality, meaning it does not meet or exceed the Boston Terrier breed standard for health, temperament, or appearance. Puppies are generally sold on a first-come, first-serve basis with little regard for the future welfare or living conditions of the dogs.

Purchasing a Boston Terrier from a backyard breeder is a gamble. You may pay less up front for a dog, but it is highly likely that you will pay a good deal more in bills for trainers and veterinarians—especially if the dog has serious health or temperament problems.

Rescue Organizations

Rescuing a purebred Boston Terrier is a viable option for many prospective owners. The Boston Terrier Club of America works tirelessly with a number of rescue groups across the country to place purebred Boston Terriers in loving homes. Bostons find their way into rescue organizations for a variety of reasons, including behaviour problems that many owners are unprepared to deal with, such as barking, digging, chewing, or urinating in the house.

Many wonderful Boston Terriers are given away or abandoned because of their owners' ignorance, indifference, or lack of compassion. Some Boston Terriers in rescue have been accidentally lost, while others have been relinquished by their owner or their owners' family because of illness, death, or other changes in circumstances. Occasionally, puppies will find their way into rescue, but the majority of Boston Terriers in rescue are older dogs, over one year of age. Many of them are senior dogs that are seven, eight, or nine years old and will make wonderful, loving companions.

All Bostons in rescue are evaluated carefully and placed in a foster home where they receive veterinary attention and obedience training. All dogs are loved and cared for until they can be

Being able to meet a pup's parent—or parents—will help you know what to expect about health and temperament.

placed in a permanent home.

Purebred Bostons that are adopted from rescue organizations are eligible to apply for an Indefinite Listing Privilege (ILP), which allows the owners of rescued purebreds to participate in companion events including obedience, agility, and tracking.

THE PEDIGREE

A pedigree is your Boston's family tree—a genetic blueprint that authenticates your dog's ancestry. However, it does not guarantee that your Boston has the genetic components that his pedigree might promise, including whether he is show quality or free of inherited diseases or disorders.

At the minimum, a breeder should supply you with a three-generation pedigree. This will tell you your Boston's parents, grandparents, and great grandparents. The names at the left of the pedigree are the names of the sire (father) and dam (mother) of your Boston. The top half of the pedigree tells you the registered names of your dog's sire's family. The bottom half of the pedigree tells you the registered names of your dog's dam's family.

Your puppy will most likely have a formal name that

When you purchase a purebred Boston Terrier you are entitled to certain types of paperwork. At the very least, you should receive a bill of sale and a pedigree. Most reputable breeders will provide you with a bill of sale, four- or five-generation pedigree, registration certificate, health certificate, and sales contract.

incorporates the name of the breeder's kennel. The breeder usually, but not always, comes up with the registered name. A dog's "call name" is his nickname, and you can give him any name you choose. (For example, Quiz Me's Ace in the Hole might be a dog's registered name, but he may be called simply "Ace.") The registered names on a pedigree may be preceded by the letters CH, which denote a Championship. Letters following your dog's name denote other accomplishments, such as obedience, tracking, or agility.

THE REGISTRATION APPLICATION

When a breeder registers a litter of puppies, they complete an AKC Litter Application. The form requires basic information, such as the date of birth, number of males and females born, and the registered names and numbers of the sire and dam. Once this information is sent to the AKC with

Your purebred puppy will come with a pedigree detailing his family tree.

applicable fees, the AKC sends the breeder a litter kit, which includes an Individual Registration Application for each puppy in the litter.

Individual Registration Application

When you purchase a puppy that meets the qualifications for AKC registration, you will get an individual registration application from the seller. The seller will fill out most of the application, including the sex of the puppy, color, markings, registration type (full or limited), transfer date, and the name and address of the new owner (and co-owners, if applicable.) The seller and all co-sellers of the litter must sign this form.

As the buyer, you will fill out the registered name of the dog (if the breeder or seller hasn't already done so), and sign the application. Once you have sent the form to the AKC with the applicable fees, it is permanently recorded in their computerized files. You will then receive a Registration Certificate, sometimes referred to as a Certificate of Registration.

Breeders first register their litters. You will complete your puppy's individual registration.

Full registration allows you full breeding rights—meaning you can register litters and puppies from your dog, provided that all other documents for breeding are in order. It also allows the registered dog to participate in all AKC-licensed events, including breed competitions.

Registration Certificates

A registration certificate is your Boston's birth certificate, so to speak. A country's governing kennel club, such as the American Kennel Club or Canadian Kennel Club, issues this certificate. When the ownership of your Boston is transferred from the breeder's name to yours, the transaction is entered on this certificate. A registration certificate shows the registration name and number of your dog, the breed, sex, color with appropriate markings, and date the certificate was issued. It will show the registration name and number of your dog's sire and dam, the name of the breeder, and the legal owner of the dog.

HEALTH RECORDS

When it comes to dogs, the one guarantee is that there are no guarantees about health or genetic problems. Genetics is a game of chance, like flipping a coin or rolling the dice. Reputable breeders do their best to eliminate genetic problems by having breeding stock tested for genetic problems and diseases, and will only breed those dogs that are proven clear of problems. However, they cannot guarantee with absolute certainty that a dog will not develop a specific fault or disease. The best they can do is supply you with certifications for your dog's sire and dam. This includes complete eye examinations by a canine ophthalmologist and certification from the Canine Eye Registration Foundation (CERF), a patella examination and certification by the Orthopedic Foundation for Animals (OFA), and the results of a Brainstem Auditory Evoked Response (BAER) test, which tests a dog's hearing.

For your puppy, the breeder should supply you with the results of a BAER test, which can be performed on puppies as young as 35 days of age. Puppies can also receive preliminary patella examinations as early as eight weeks of age, but they cannot be certified until at least 12 months of age. A breeder should provide you with a copy of the preliminary results. At eight weeks old, your Boston can be examined to detect congenital heritable eye defects. Once the puppy's eyes are examined, the breeder can send the results in and obtain certification from CERF. This is not a lifetime certification, though. Annual examinations are recommended because the health of the eyes can change from one year to the next.

Responsible breeders test their breeding stock to try to ensure their puppies are as healthy as possible.

A breeder should also supply you with a record of your Boston's inoculations and worming schedule along with any veterinary treatment.

BILL OF SALE

You should receive from the breeder a bill of sale in the form of a registration application or a signed statement that you own the dog. A bill of sale will usually include the puppy's name, sex, color, date whelped, and the name of the puppy's sire and dam. It should include the date of sale, your name, address, and telephone number. It should also include the name and address of the breeder, the purchase price of the Boston Terrier, and the date you bought and took possession of the puppy.

It may also include specific information or guarantees relating to the puppy. For example, it might say that the puppy has been raised under sanitary conditions, and to the best of the breeder's knowledge the puppy is in excellent health and is guaranteed free from communicable diseases. It might also include contractual information regarding the puppy, such as who is responsible for veterinary attention, and the breeder's return policy. Oftentimes, these types of terms are stipulated in a puppy sales contract.

The contract will usually state if the dog is to be spayed or neutered and, if so, a reasonable time frame in which it must be done. Some breeders offer an incentive in the form of a rebate or partial refund once veterinary certification has been received. Some breeders will hold onto registration papers until they receive veterinary proof of spaying or neutering.

The contract should stipulate the conditions under which you are entitled to a full, partial, or zero refund for the dog. For example, if you change your mind, there is usually a time limit on certain guarantees, usually 48 or 72 hours, because exposure to health hazards, such as disease, injury, emotional trauma, and abuse are all out of the breeder's control. A contract can specify that the buyer will have the dog examined by a veterinarian within a set time—again, usually 24 to 48 hours. This is done to establish a record of health. It also helps to detect any possible or potential problems that might arise.

Any hereditary problems that would require replacement of a puppy, such as patella or eye problems, commonly require appropriate documentation in the form of a veterinarian's statement, OFA evaluation, or an eye certification from a certified canine ophthalmologist. This is especially important in cases of genetic defects that are not apparent until later in the dog's life. It is not unreasonable for a breeder to require the necessary documentation to substantiate the claim. Who pays for these tests should be stipulated in the sales contract.

Sales contracts can include or exclude an enormous amount of information. Before signing any documents, read them carefully and be sure you understand all of the terms and conditions. It is always prudent to seek legal advice before signing contracts and legally binding documents.

PREPARING YOUR HOME

Once you've made your selection, be it male or female, puppy or adult, pet or show dog, you are now owned by a Boston Terrier. Your life is about to be transformed! Be prepared for a journey filled with happiness, laughter, and unconditional love.

To make the transition as smooth as possible, there are certain things you should do before bringing your new Boston Terrier home. Much of this information is geared toward preparing your home for a new puppy, but can also be applied to an adult dog. It is worth mentioning that when you obtain an adult dog whose background and training are a bit sketchy, such as a rescue dog, it is always a good idea to assume the dog has no training and begin his training as if he were a puppy.

Puppy Proofing

It is best to puppy-proof your house before your puppy arrives. This includes anything your puppy is likely to seek out and destroy. Like toddlers, puppies will want to explore their surroundings and will try to put everything in their

Once you and your family have selected your puppy (or dog), expect your life to be transformed.

mouth—whether it fits or not. Your puppy is too young to understand that your expensive Italian loafers are not for teething. Pick up shoes, books, magazines, and pillows. Put all houseplants, prescription bottles, wastebaskets, and candy dishes up out of reach. Tuck electrical cords behind furniture, under rugs, or tape them to the baseboards. Do not leave cigarette butts in ashtrays, as they can cause nicotine poisoning. Many objects, if swallowed, such as shoelaces, buttons, socks, marbles, paperclips, and dismembered GI Joe dolls, can cause life-threatening intestinal blockage, and surgery may be required to remove the offending object.

You will also need to puppy-proof your yard, garden, and outdoor areas. This includes picking up hoses, sprinklers, poisonous plants, and lawn ornaments that your puppy is likely to chew on when left unsupervised. Antifreeze is highly attractive to dogs and deadly if ingested. Be sure to store containers of poisonous products—antifreeze, fertilizers, weed and insect killers—on shelves where they are safely out of reach of inquisitive, thrill-seeking Boston Terriers.

Make sure there are no gaps or holes in fencing or secret passageways in your garden that a Boston is likely to escape through. If your property is not fenced, be sure your puppy is on a leash each and every time he goes outdoors. He does not have the mental wherewithal to understand that the street is a dangerous place to be. It is your job to keep him safe.

DOGGY ESSENTIALS

You will need basic doggie essentials including a leash, collar, food, food and water bowls, crate, dog bed, ID tag, and an assortment of training toys and chew toys. From a practical standpoint, your Boston will survive just fine without the designer clothes, rhinestone-studded collar and matching leash, canine cologne, and a faux-fur bone-shaped bed, but what's the point of having a Boston Terrier if you can't indulge his chic canine sense of style?

A Crate

Crates come in different shapes, sizes, and materials, with each offering their own advantages. Some are folding, wire crates that provide good air circulation and help keep dogs cool when temperatures begin to rise. A variety of crate covers can turn any wire crate into a secure den and provide protection from the elements. Other crate types include heavy-duty, high-impact plastic kennels that meet domestic and international airline requirements for airline travel. Folding crates such as those made by Nylabone have the added value and convenience of being easy to store away when not in use. There's also a variety of soft canvas and water-resistant–type crates that are ideal for home and travel. They are easy to set up and take down

An exercise pen (ex-pen) can keep your dogs safely confined in a small space indoors or out and allows for them to see out easily and get lots of air.

and, as an added bonus, are often machine washable. Some come equipped with a myriad of extra features, such as zippered sides, storage pockets, carry bags, and wheels.

While the initial expense may seem high, a good-quality crate will last a lifetime, and the benefits definitely make it well worth the cost. It's certainly cheaper than replacing damaged carpet and furniture six months down the road.

Exercise Pen

Like a crate, an exercise pen or playpen is indispensable for raising a well-behaved puppy. They are ideal to place anywhere you need a temporary kennel area, such as the kitchen or family room. Like a crate, it is essential for safely confining your Boston when you cannot give him your undivided attention. For instance, when you are preparing supper, chatting on the phone, or paying bills.

It is also helpful during those times when you are overly tired or getting a bit frustrated with your Boston. These short periods of alone time give you a chance to recoup and help to teach your Boston some self-control. He will learn to lie down, relax, and be by himself for short periods of time without making a fuss or getting anxious or neurotic.

Beds

Your Boston Terrier puppy will need a bed of his own, but it is best to hold off on the ultra deluxe model until he is well through the chewing stage. A tenacious chewer can turn a posh canine bed into worthless confetti in the time it takes you to unload the groceries. A large blanket or towel folded over several times or a cozy fleece pad placed in his crate or exercise pen will do the job for the first few months. These are easily cleaned in the washing machine and therefore less likely to develop that distinctive *doggie* smell.

Head Collars

If you have a Boston who is a nuisance puller for whom your best training efforts haven't succeeded and you worry about pulling too hard on his neck (as you should), you might consider a head halter, depending on your level of patience. A head halter goes over your dog's face and applies pressure to the back of the neck rather than the front of the throat. While they can be very effective, most dogs are not used to this type of configuration, and it can require a great deal of preconditioning, patience, and diligence in order to make it a positive experience for your Boston.

Collars

Choosing a collar for your thick-necked, flat-faced Boston should not present too many challenges. There are many different types and styles of collars from which to choose, and they are generally made of leather, nylon, cotton, or hemp. They also come in a variety of styles: buckle, harness, head halter, half-check, greyhound, choke chain, slip chain, and martingale.

Being a brachycephalic breed, Boston Terriers are prone to respiratory and breathing problems. They are also sensitive to rough treatment, harsh training methods, and tracheal collapse, which make the choke chain or half-check collars less than an ideal choice. If, however, you decide to go with either of these collars, always seek professional advice from a knowledgeable trainer. When used incorrectly, they can cause serious physical and psychological damage to your Boston.

A good choice is a flat, lightweight nylon buckle collar. They are relatively inexpensive and available at retail pet stores. A flat, lightweight leather or rolled leather collar is more expensive, but when properly cared for, it will last a lifetime. There are significant differences in the quality of leather collars, so if this is your preference, be sure to select a high-quality leather

A properly fitted collar will not only look stylish on your dog, it is a necessary piece of equipment for him.

collar from a reputable manufacturer.

Martingale-type leashes work on a loop-on-loop system, which creates a limited amount of closure and pressure, so they are safer than traditional choke chains. They are ideal for Boston Terriers that do not pull on their leashes while walking.

If you aren't interested in obedience competition and are happy as long as your Boston is in the general vicinity of heel position, a harness might be the solution. A harness will not keep your Boston from pulling, but it will take the pressure off his trachea. As there are a variety of models available in different shapes, sizes, and materials, it is best to seek professional advice in order to correctly fit your Boston Terrier with a harness and avoid a problem with chafing.

Whichever option you choose, it is important that your Boston always wear a buckle collar with identification. This is his ticket home should he become lost or separated from you.

Leashes

Like collars, leashes come in a variety of choices and their selection is usually just a matter of personal preference. Nylon leashes are lightweight and relatively inexpensive, so you won't be too distraught if you misplace them. They come in every color of the rainbow and can even be personalized with your name and telephone number. Some are durable enough to withstand multiple trips through the washing machine.

Leather leashes are a bit more costly but often worth the investment. A good-quality, well-cared for leather leash will be around long after your Boston has settled into his golden years. Some owners find leather leads to be easier on their hands than their nylon counterparts. Again, it comes down to personal preference.

This Boston Terrier has everything he needs—a collar, a leash, a bandana for extra appeal, a favorite toy, and a spot in the shade!

Retractable leads are designed to extend and retract at the touch of a button. They allow you to give your Boston plenty of distance on walks without carrying a long line that can get tangled, dragged through the mud, or wrapped around bushes. A retractable lead that extends to 16 feet allows your Boston plenty of privacy to do his business or explore an open field while you lag behind. A single finger-brake button allows you to stop your dog at any time. Retractable leads are also ideal for teaching and reinforcing the come command. If you go this route, be sure to invest in a good quality retractable lead, which should last a lifetime.

Identification Tags

I.D. tags that include your dog's name and your telephone number are a must for all dogs. They are relatively inexpensive and well worth the investment. They are your Boston's ticket home should he become lost or separated. Tags are readily available at retail pet outlets, through mail order catalogs, and from online vendors. They come in a variety of shapes, sizes, colors, and materials, and easily attach to your dog's buckle collar with an S clip or good-quality split ring. Nameplates attach directly to your dog's collar—not unlike the brass nameplates used on a horse's halter—and eliminate the unmistakable, not to mention frequently annoying, jingling noise produced by multiple tags dangling from a dog's collar.

Food Dishes

Your dog might consider these the most important on your list of supplies for him. Afterall, mealtimes are some of a dog's best times, and you'll want to be sure your puppy or dog has bowls for both food and water.

Like the other doggy essentials, there are plenty of bowls to choose from, and you can have a lot of fun with the selection. A couple of things to keep in mind to make everyone's lives healthier and easier, though. The bowls you select should be easy to clean, should not slip when they are placed on the floor, and should be made of a material that is not potentially harmful. To meet these criteria you should focus on stainless steel or heavy ceramic bowls—so long as the ceramic is finished with non-toxic glaze. The stainless steel is especially easy to clean, and most models come with rubber on the bottom to keep them from sliding.

As mentioned, you'll need two bowls: one for water, and one for food. You must have a bowl of clean, fresh water available for your Boston at all times. Rinse the bowl and refill several times a day, and thoroughly clean it at least once a day. Your dog's food bowl should be cleaned before and after his regular meals.

When choosing an engraved disc or nameplate, be sure to check it on a regular basis for readability. Stainless steel, brass, or gold-plated tags allow for deep engraving and maintain readability longer. Barrel-type identification tags allow you to write information on a piece of paper and insert it into the barrel that attaches to your dog's collar. When choosing this type of ID tag, be certain the barrel cannot come apart, causing your dog's information to become lost.

Identification tags come in different shapes, sizes, and colors to suit you and your animal. All provide the protection of added security. A microchip is another safe (and permanent) form of identification.

The Miracle of Microchips

Until recently, tattooing was the most widely used method of permanently identifying an animal. Now technology has given dog owners peace of mind in the form of a microchip. It is a silicon chip, also called a transponder, about the size of a grain of rice that is inserted under your dog's skin. The microchip contains an unalterable identification number, which is recorded on a central database along with your name, address, and telephone number. The microchip is scanned and the identification number is read via a hand-held electronic scanner. A universal scanner introduced in the United States in 1996 can now detect and read the numbers of all major brands of microchips. A microchip won't do your Boston Terrier any good if it's not registered. Several state and national registries are available for registering and storing your contact information.

Toys

Bostons, like all dogs, not only enjoy chewing, they need to chew. Especially puppies, who will experience teething as their baby teeth erupt and fall out. Again, there is a vast and seemingly endlessly entertaining selection of dog toys available, and you and your Boston can have a lot of fun selecting favorites. Your healthiest and most long-lasting selections, however, will be toys made for your Boston's body type and chewing power. Hard nylon and rubber toys are made for real gnawing and gnashing. They exercise your dog's teeth and gums, promoting oral health while relieving the need to chew. You can learn more about the best types of these toys for your Boston on the Nylabone website.

Age- and breed-appropriate chew toys will keep your Boston's need to chew satisfied.

Be careful with plush toys that contain squeakers or noise-makers. Some Bostons will chew right through the material and may swallow the squeaker, which could become lodged in their throat.

There are also many kinds of edible chews and toys for dogs now that provide nutritional enhancement or breath fresheners. Most are strong enough for Bostons to get a good chew out of before breaking into bits that can be eaten. These shouldn't be substitutes for the more long-lasting chew toys, but they make an enjoyable break for your dog.

PET SITTING, DOGGIE DAYCARE, AND BOARDING

There are countless reasons why your precious pooch might be excluded from your travel plans. There are unexpected business trips or family emergencies, and not all hotels, motels, and resorts accept dogs—even well-behaved Boston Terriers. You might be flying a significant distance. The weather may be too hot or too cold for your Boston. Whatever the reason, occasions may arise when you need to leave your Boston for a few days or a few weeks. There are several options that can give you peace of mind when leaving your Boston behind.

Boarding Facilities

Boarding facilities have come a long way in the last 10 or 15 years. Many are designed with the discriminating pet owner in mind. They offer enticing names—K-9 Bed and Breakfast, Canine Condo, Pet Resort—and they provide a variety of services in addition to boarding, such as training, daily exercise, and grooming.

Your Boston's physical safety and emotional well being are paramount. Here are some tips for reducing yours and your Boston's stress by choosing the best facility:

- Visit and tour the entire facility. A clean and inviting reception area does not guarantee clean kennel runs. If the proprietors do not want you touring the facility—hightail it to the nearest exit.
- Check the cleanliness of the kennels, runs, and exercise areas. Are they free of debris and excrement? How often are the kennels cleaned? How are they cleaned and disinfected between boarders? Does the kennel or

exercise area smell?

- Check the security of the facility. Is it completely fenced? Double fenced? Do the kennels and exercise yards have good latches? Are the fences sturdy and at least six feet high?
- Where will your Boston be boarded? Indoors? Outdoors? Or a combination of the two? Are the indoor facilities heated? Are the outdoor facilities protected from the weather?
- What will your Boston be sleeping on? Do you need to bring his bed or favorite blanket?
- If you have several Bostons, can you kennel them together? Is there an additional cost to do so?
- How frequently will your Boston be walked or exercised? For how long? What type of exercise? Does someone interact or play with him? Or is he simply left unattended in an exercise yard with or without other dogs?
- Is there a veterinarian or 24-hour emergency clinic nearby?
- What are their admission and pick-up hours? What happens if your return is delayed?
- What vaccinations are required?

Once you have decided on a facility, remember to book early. Many facilities are booked months in advance, especially during the holidays. Always leave special pet-care instructions, your itinerary, and numbers to contact you or a trusted friend or relative in the event of an emergency.

Pet Sitters

If the mere thought of boarding your Boston is enough to break your heart and your Boston's, you might want to consider a pet sitter. He may still be heartbroken that you are gone, but it is likely he'll be less stressed in the comfort of his own home surrounded by his prized possessions. Most likely, he'll be happier sticking to his normal routine, or as close to normal as possible, eating his regular diet, sleeping in his own bed, playing with his beloved toys, and lounging in his favorite spot. If you have a responsible neighbor, trusted friend, or relative you can rely on to stop by several times a day—count your blessings!

In some areas, professional pet sitters are available. These are people that either stay at your home while you are gone or stop in during the day to feed, exercise, and check on your Boston. Ask your dog-owning friends, local veterinarians, trainers, or groomers for a referral. You can also check with Pet Sitters International or the National Association of Professional Pet Sitters.

Doggie Daycare

Doggie daycare is similar to pet sitting but with a twist. Similar to daycare centers for human babies and toddlers, doggie daycare centers are for owners who want their precious pooches to play, interact, romp, and tussle with other dogs while they are at work.

To find the right daycare facility for your Boston, consider the following:

- Always visit and tour the facility.
- What type of services do they provide?
- What type of supervision do they have? How many dogs are assigned to each person?
- What safety precautions are taken?
- Are puppies and small dogs separated from large puppies and dogs?
- Are quiet, timid dogs separated from rambunctious, overzealous dogs?

- Do they have a place for your Boston to get away from the other dogs?
- What type of training or experience do the dog handlers have?
- Where will your Boston spend his day? Indoors? Outdoors? In play groups?
- What vaccinations and shots are required?
- Is there a veterinarian or emergency clinic nearby?

Once you have decided on a daycare facility, always leave a telephone number where you or a trusted friend or family member can be reached in the event of an emergency.

TRAVELING WITH YOUR BOSTON

Boston Terriers are always up for fun, especially if the agenda includes spending time with their owners or accompanying them on vacation. Most Boston Terriers are adaptable and make wonderful travelers, but don't wait until you are on the road to discover that yours is not! Ideally, it is best to accustom your Boston to traveling while he is young. Whether you have a puppy or an adult dog, it is best to begin with short trips around the block, to the market, bank, and so forth. Each time gradually increase the distance, making the experience fun and positive. You can put a favorite blanket, toy, or treat in his crate to keep him comfy and occupied. Remember, traveling with a Boston is not unlike traveling with a small child. You will need to make frequent pit stops to allow him to relieve himself, stretch his legs, and burn off a bit of pent-up energy.

Travel Checklist for Your Boston

Once your suitcase is packed, it's time to pack your dog's necessities:
- Your Boston's health certificate and rabies inoculation.
- Current photographs of your dog, to be used for identification should he become lost.
- An extra leash, collar, and set of ID tags.
- An adequate supply of food, water, and feeding dishes.
- A pooper-scooper, paper towels, or plastic bags for picking up after your Boston.
- First-aid kit containing antibiotic ointment, hydrogen peroxide, gauze strips, specific medications and prescriptions.
- Chew toys, bones, tug toys, balls, and the like.
- A travel kennel or pet carrier.
- A favorite blanket or bed.
- An adequate supply of doggie towels for quick cleanups, in case your Boston gets wet, dirty, sick, or injured.
- Grooming tools, such as brush, comb, shampoo, and nail clippers.

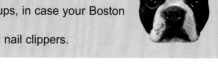

FEEDING
YOUR BOSTON TERRIER

N o doubt you've heard the old adage, "You are what you eat." The same concept applies to your Boston Terrier. Feeding a complete and balanced diet is the first step in providing your dog with the necessary nutrients to live a happy, healthy life. Studies indicate that proper nutrition can help prevent disease, promote healthy skin and coat, and provide your Boston Terrier with optimum health and longevity. While a trip to the pet food aisle can seem more intimidating than learning computer science, feeding your four-legged friend a well-balanced diet is nothing to be afraid of: all it really requires is a basic understanding of canine nutrition, a keen observation of your Boston and whether or not his diet is agreeing with him, and, finally, the ability to look beyond the slick multimillion-dollar ad campaigns.

THE BASICS

When it comes to nutrition, all dogs are not created equal. Some dogs have allergies to certain food sources, such as beef, chicken, or fish, which can cause a wide variety of problems. Some dogs are sensitive to or intolerant of poor-quality ingredients and grain-based diets. Bostons, as a breed, are prone to flatulence, and that is one condition you definitely don't want to make worse! Because the Boston is a short-faced breed, it may have trouble picking up, chewing, and swallowing a large-size kibble or dry food. The breed is also prone to dental overcrowding, and feeding a strictly canned food diet may promote a faster accumulation of plaque and tartar.

One of the most important requirements in feeding your Boston is to look at his individual nutritional needs, and then feed him a diet that provides the correct combination of nutrients. What works for one Boston may not work for another because a dog's nutritional needs will change depending on his age, environment, housing conditions, overall health, and the emotional and physical demands you put on him. A canine athlete competing in performance events will require a different diet than a canine couch potato. If your Boston's main job is guarding the couch, it is likely he will not require as many calories as a full-time show dog that is dealing with the rigors of campaigning. A pregnant or lactating bitch's nutritional requirements will differ from that of a ten-year-old spayed Boston.

Each dog is unique; it's your job to provide your Boston with the best possible diet.

To help your Boston Terrier's complex system run efficiently, it is important to find the diet that provides the correct balance of nutrients for his individual requirements.

It is highly likely that your Boston's diet will change several times over the course of his lifetime. However, the foundation of canine nutrition remains the same. There are six basic elements of nutrition: water, minerals, vitamins, fats, proteins, and carbohydrates.

Water

One seldom thinks of water as an essential nutrient. However, it is the single most important nutrient needed to sustain your four-legged friend's health. In addition to regulating your Boston's body temperature--which is highly important because Bostons are prone to overheating--water plays an important part in supporting metabolic reactions and acts as the transportation system, so to speak, that allows blood to carry vital nutritional materials to the cells, and remove waste products from your dog's system.

Rather than trying to estimate your Boston's daily water requirement, it is best to provide him with access to an abundant supply of fresh, cool drinking water at all times.

Always have clean, cool water available for your dog—it's a critical nutrient!

When dogs have free access to water, they will normally drink enough to maintain the proper balance of body fluids. If you have concerns about the quality of your city water or about fluoride, chlorine, or lead in your water supply, consider a filtration system or try boiling water or purchasing bottled water for your Boston.

It is worth noting that infectious agents and diseases, such as leptospirosis, Giardia, and E.coli can be transmitted through contaminated water. To greatly reduce the risk of disease, it is prudent not to allow your Boston to drink from puddles, streams, or ponds, as the water could be contaminated with parasites that could make him ill.

Minerals

Not too many people get excited about minerals. You seldom hear diet gurus fawning over minerals like they do with fats, carbohydrates, and proteins. Minerals do not yield sources of energy, but they are important in the overall nutritional equation because they help regulate your Boston's complex system and are crucial components in energy metabolism.

Minerals are classified as micro minerals or macro minerals depending on their concentration in the body. Micro minerals, or trace elements, include iodine, iron, copper, cobalt, zinc, manganese, molybdenum, fluorine, and chromium, which dogs need in very small amounts. Macro minerals are needed in large quantities and include sodium, potassium, magnesium, calcium, and phosphorous.

Essential nutrients are those that your Boston must obtain from food because his body cannot make them in sufficient quantity to meet his physiological needs. If dogs get too much or too little of a specific mineral in their diets, it can upset the delicate balance and cause serious health problems including tissue damage, convulsions, increased heart rate, and anemia. You should never attempt to supplement minerals in your Boston's diet without professional advice from a veterinarian.

Vitamins

A dog's body does not extract usable energy from vitamins, but they are essential as helpers in the metabolic processes. Vitamins are vital to your Boston's health and areavailable in food sources, but they can be easily destroyed in the cooking and processing of commercial dog foods. Certain vitamins are dependent on one another, with nearly every action in a dog's body requiring the assistance of vitamins. Vitamin deficiencies and/or excesses can lead to serious health problems, such as anorexia, artery and vein degeneration, dehydration, muscle weakness, and impairment of motor control and balance.

Vitamins fall into two categories: water-soluble (B-complex and vitamin C) and fat-soluble (A, D, E, and K.) Unlike humans, dogs can make vitamin C from glucose, so they do not need to acquire it in their diet. All other water-soluble vitamins must be replenished on a regular basis through diet. Fat-soluble vitamins are absorbed and stored in the body, which makes over-supplementation potentially dangerous. Seek your veterinarian's advice and read as much as you can before supplementing your dog's food.

Carbohydrates

Dogs are omnivores, meaning they eat both animal and vegetable foods, and they get most of their energy from carbohydrates. Carbohydrates are the energy foods that fuel your Boston's body. Scientific research indicates that up to 50 percent of an adult dog's diet can come from carbohydrates. They are often referred to as *protein-sparing* nutrients because the action of carbohydrates (and fats) in providing energy allows protein to be used for its own unique roles.

Soluble carbohydrates consist mainly of starches and sugars and are easily digested. Insoluble carbohydrates, better known as fiber, resist enzymatic digestion in the small intestine. Fiber, while important to the overall process, is not an essential nutrient.

Carbohydrates are introduced in the diet primarily through vegetable matter, legumes, and cereal grains, such as rice, wheat, corn, barley, and oats. Unused carbohydrates are stored in the body as converted fat and as glycogen in the muscles and liver. In the absence of adequate carbohydrates, your Boston's system is able to utilize fat and protein as a form of energy. However, protein is less efficient because the body does not make a specialized storage form of protein, as it does for fats and carbohydrates. When protein is used as an energy source—rather than doing its unique job of building muscle, regulating body functions, and so forth—the body

must dismantle its valuable tissue proteins and use them for energy.

Many dog treats are grain-based, making them sources of high amounts of carbohydrates.

Protein

Proteins are compounds of carbon, hydrogen, oxygen, and nitrogen atoms arranged into a string of amino acids—much like the pearls on a necklace. Amino acids are the building blocks of life because they build vital proteins that build strong muscles, ligaments, organs, bones, teeth, and coat. Protein also defends the body against disease, and is critical when it comes to the repair and maintenance of all the body's tissue, hormones, enzymes, electrolyte balances, and antibodies.

There are ten essential amino acids that your Boston's body cannot make on its own or make in sufficient quantities. These amino acids must be obtained through his diet. To make protein, a cell must have all of the needed amino acids available simultaneously because the body makes complete proteins only. If one amino acid is missing, the other amino acids cannot form a partial protein. If complete proteins are not formed, it reduces and limits the body's ability to grow and repair tissue.

Fats are an essential part of a balanced diet, so don't purposely deprive your Boston of them. On the other hand, don't feed them in excess.

Fats

Fats and oils are the most concentrated sources of food energy in your Boston's diet. They play an important role in contributing to your dog's healthy skin and coat and aid in the absorption, transport, and storage of fat-soluble vitamins. Fats also increase the palatability of foods, but they contain more than twice the calories of protein and carbohydrates. Just like your own diet, fats in your Boston's diet should be regulated because consuming too much fat can result in excess calorie intake, which is not good for your Boston's health or "waistline."

HOMEMADE DIETS

Let's face it, unless you are an experienced canine nutritionist with an abundance of time and energy on your hands, feeding a homemade diet is easier said than done. Preparing your Boston's food from scratch is a romantic and selfless notion. After all, who doesn't want the best for their dog? Who doesn't want to know exactly what ingredients are going in their Boston's stomach? What owner doesn't want to feed foods free of preservatives, additives, and who knows what else?

Truth be told, homemade diets require a time-consuming, labor-intensive, and complicated process. It is tricky, albeit not impossible, to prepare a canine diet on a routine daily basis that is complete and balanced and contains the proper ratio of nutrients. Supplementing nutrients is an alternative, but that can be harmful to your dog, too. The bottom line is that when you choose to feed a homemade diet, you assume full responsibility for the nutritional status of your Boston. If this is what you decide to do, it is prudent to consult with your veterinarian or a certified veterinary nutritionist before proceeding.

BONES & RAW FOOD DIETS

It is not difficult to find proponents and opponents on both sides of the controversial issue of whether a BARF (bones and raw food) diet is best for dogs. Ask a dozen people and each one is sure to have a different opinion. Essentially, some owners believe that raw bones and foods are more suitable for their dog than highly processed foods because they believe drying, freezing, heating, or canning robs food of its nutritional components. The concept appears to stem from the desire to return to a more *natural* style of living and to feed a *pure* diet, similar to what wild dogs might have eaten long ago.

There are two challenges with this type of diet: First, it is difficult finding a good source of healthy raw meat and bones, and then achieving the correct balance of nutrients— water, vitamins, minerals, protein, carbohydrates, fats—in the right amounts, and doing so on a routine basis. Second, dogs that eat raw bones, particularly chicken and turkey bones, are highly susceptible to choking or damaging their stomachs. Both of these situations can be life threatening. In addition, parasites are a concern because dogs, like humans, are susceptible to internal parasites, bacteria, and food-borne illnesses caused by raw meat, poultry, eggs, and unprocessed milk.

COMMERCIAL DIETS

Commercial diets are those we see on store shelves around the world. They are undoubtedly the most convenient foods to buy, store, and use. They are readily available, and when compared to homemade diets, they tend to be less

time consuming to prepare. Most major dog food manufacturers, and a number of veterinary hospitals, have invested enormous sums of money in researching and studying the nutritional requirements of dogs in different stages of life. As a result, they now know more about the requirements of puppies, adult dogs, athletic dogs, pregnant bitches, and senior dogs, and what constitutes good canine nutrition.

It is also important to keep in mind that the commercial dog food industry is a multibillion-dollar-a-year business. Advertising experts spend a significant amount of time researching, developing, and marketing products to convince you to buy a particular brand. This isn't necessarily bad, but it is important to keep in mind if you're choosing a food because of the creative advertisements and fancy packaging rather than the nutritional requirements of your dog.

Premium vs Cost-Conscious Foods

There is no substitute for good nutrition. For maximum health and longevity, a dog must be properly fed and cared for throughout his life. Choosing a premium food over a bargain or generic brand food makes good nutritional and economic sense. Across the board, premium foods tend to be nutritionally complete, meaning they have all the required nutrients in balanced proportions, so your Boston is getting adequate amounts of all required nutrients. Premium foods are also developed to provide optimal nutrition for dogs during different stages of life, such as puppy, maintenance, active, and senior diets. The initial investment for a premium food is a bit higher on a per weight basis, but because they tend to be higher in digestibility and nutrient availability, less food is required per serving.

Forms & Formulations

Commercial foods tend to be classified into food types: dry, canned, and semi-moist. Frozen and dehydrated foods

Commercially manufactured dog foods are convenient, practical, and nutritionally sound for most dogs. However, you are your dog's guardian and must decide ultimately what's best for him.

are also becoming increasingly popular in the competitive dog food market.

Dry Food

Dry foods, commonly called "kibble," contain between six to ten percent moisture (water) and a high percentage of carbohydrates in the form of grains.

Advantages

- Economical, readily available, and convenient to buy, store, and use.
- Good shelf life. Does not require refrigeration.
- May improve dental hygiene through chewing and grinding, which aids in the removal of dental plaque. (Does not eliminate the need for regular dental care.)
- Provides some exercise for a dog's mouth, and helps satisfy a puppy's need to chew.
- High-quality brands have high caloric density and good digestibility, which means lower amounts per serving need to be consumed.

Bargain or generic brand foods tend to have lower levels of digestibility and nutrient availability than premium brands. They may or may not provide a complete and balanced diet. Overall, they tend to be less expensive to buy, but you will have to provide larger servings to realize the nutrient density and availability of the more costly premium brands.

- Stool is usually smaller and more compact.

Disadvantages
- Less palatable to some dogs than canned or semi-moist foods.
- High heats used in the processing stage can destroy valuable nutrients.

Semi-Moist Foods

Semi-moist foods are often shaped into patties and come in a prepackaged size convenient for feeding. They are generally marketed in sealed and resealable pouches. They are 25 to 35 percent water, which is a higher percentage than dry foods. Ingredients can include fresh or frozen animal tissues, cereal grains, fats, and simple sugars. It is worth noting that semi-moist foods contain propylene glycol, which is an odorless, tasteless, slightly syrupy liquid used to make antifreeze and de-icing products. Propylene glycol is generally recognized as safe by the FDA for use in dog food and other animal feeds. It is used to absorb extra water and maintain moisture, and as a solvent for food coloring and flavor.

Advantages
- High sugar content may increase palatability.
- Less offensive smelling than canned foods.
- Good shelf life. Does not require refrigeration.

Disadvantages
- High sugar levels in dog food causes spikes in blood sugar levels and contributes to obesity.
- High sugar levels may aggravate an existing or borderline diabetic condition.
- Contains high levels of salt.
- Contains propylene glycol.
- Sticky, sugary foods can contribute to dental disease.
- If left out for long periods of time, such as in a dog bowl, it will dry out, reducing palatability.

Moist (Canned) Foods

Canned foods are mostly water: approximately 75 percent. They contain more meat than a dry diet and little to no grain.

Advantages
- High palatability.
- Easier to digest.
- Contains a higher meat protein level.

- Canning process kills harmful bacteria.
- Long shelf life.

Disadvantages
- More expensive than dry foods.
- Provides no abrasion from chewing, so allows faster plaque and tartar buildup on teeth.
- Requires refrigeration after opening.
- High-heat processing can destroy some nutrients.
- Due to high water content, moist foods have fewer nutrients than other foods. More food must be eaten to satisfy energy and nutrient needs.

Dehydrated Foods

Dehydrated foods, which contain fresh meats, grains, and vegetables, are dehydrated at low temperatures to preserve all the natural nutrients.

Advantages
- Once dehydrated, foods can last indefinitely.
- Easy to store.

Disadvantages
- Can be costly.
- When rehydrated the food becomes a moist mixture.
- Does not provide abrasion or scraping while chewing.

FEEDING PUPPIES

A Boston puppy has significant nutritional demands. Besides the fact that a puppy spends much of his day playing, which requires a lot of calories, his body is growing rapidly. His system is building strong muscles, bones, and vital organs, and establishing a resistance to disease. As a result, for the first 12 months of his life he needs a specially formulated growth food that is designed exclusively for his greater energy and nutritional needs.

A growing puppy needs about twice as many calories per kilogram of body weight as an adult Boston. Since puppies have small stomachs, they also need to be fed smaller amounts of food three or four times a day until they are about six months old. From six months to one year of age and thereafter, you should feed your Boston two times a day—once in the morning and again in the evening.

Growth rates and appetites of puppies are primarily dictated by genetics and will vary from puppy to puppy, so

Puppies need to be fed several times a day to meet their increased energy needs.

feeding the correct amount can be a bit tricky. The feeding guidelines on dog foods are just that—guidelines. They are not etched in stone. Many dog food manufacturers tend to be overly generous with their proportions. Your veterinarian can help you determine the proper amount to feed.

For the first few days after bringing your precious pooch home, you should continue feeding the same type and brand of puppy food he has been eating, provided he has been eating a well-balanced, good-quality puppy food. Depending on where and from whom you purchase your Boston, this may or may not be the case.

If you intend to switch foods, it is best to do so slowly to prevent intestinal upset. Veterinarians recommend switching foods over the course of seven to ten days to prevent upset stomachs, vomiting, loose stool, or constipation. To do this, make a mixture of 75 percent *old* food and 25 percent *new* food. Feed this mixture for three or four days. Then make a mixture of 50 percent *old* food and 50 percent *new* food. Feed this mixture for three or four days. Then make a mixture of 25 percent old food and 75 percent new food. Feed this mixture for three or four days. Then you can start feeding 100 percent new food.

In addition, you will need to feed your puppy at regular times. Whatever food is left after 15 minutes should be picked up and, if necessary, refrigerated or thrown away. This regimen will help your puppy establish a regular routine of eating and eliminating, which will help speed up the house-training process. Designated feeding times can also help with the bonding process.

Free-feeding, which is putting the food down and leaving it out all day, allowing your puppy to eat at his leisure, is not recommended, because it does not establish a set schedule for feeding and eliminating. While a few dogs are able to regulate their food intake, most dogs will eat and eat and eat as long as food is available. They eat until they make themselves sick, and then they gleefully start all over again. If food is perpetually available, some dogs will develop the annoying and potentially dangerous habit of food-bowl guarding. Finally, if you have multiple dogs, you will not know for certain whether your puppy is eating or if the other dogs are eating for him.

FEEDING AN ADULT

Different breeds of dogs reach maturity at different ages. As a general rule, smaller breeds tend to reach adulthood sooner than large-breed dogs. It is highly likely your Boston Terrier will reach adulthood between 9 and 12 months of age. That said, the age of maturity varies from Boston to Boston, with some Boston Terriers reaching maturity sooner or later than others.

Adult foods, often called maintenance diets, are specially designed foods that satisfy the energy and nutritional needs of adult dogs that have reached maturity. These diets are designed to provide the proper quantities of nutrients to support a mature Boston's lifestyle. Bostons that are very active or under physical or emotional stress, as well as pregnant females, have different nutrient requirements than the average canine couch potato. Your veterinarian can help you determine when and what type of adult food to choose. Most experts recommend feeding an adult dog twice a day—once in the morning and again in the early evening. As with puppies, pick up any food left after 15 minutes and either refrigerate it or throw it away.

Feeding the Senior Boston

The average lifespan of a Boston Terrier is between 9 and

If your dog has healthy skin, a lustrous itch-free coat, bright eyes, and a normal energy level, the diet you're feeding is doing its job.

12 years of age. Different dogs age at different rates, and determining if and when you should begin feeding a senior food will depend on your individual dog. It is impossible to arbitrarily set an *old-age* age. You cannot randomly say that Bostons are old at six or seven years of age. Dogs age differently, depending on their genetics and overall lifestyle.

That said, a good rule of thumb is to divide the average lifespan of a Boston into thirds. When your Boston is in the last third of his life, he is usually considered an older or senior dog. Using that simplified mathematical equation, the average Boston would be considered an older dog around six and a half or seven years of age. Again, there are exceptions to every rule and some Bostons remain physically and cognitively young at eight or nine years of age.

Older dogs usually require a diet that is still complete and well balanced, yet lower in calories, protein, and fat. In some instances, you may be able to feed your Boston his regular adult food but in lower quantities. Or you may need to switch to a diet designed specifically for senior dogs.

On the other side of the spectrum, older dogs will occasionally go off of their food, meaning they lose interest in it, and may choose to eat only once a day. If your Boston is losing weight and not eating well, it is important that he be checked by a veterinarian to rule out any possible illness.

Because dogs age at different rates, it is best to work closely with a veterinarian as your Boston Terrier begins to enter his senior years. Your veterinarian can help you determine the specific nutritional and supplemental needs of your Boston in this stage of his life.

SUPPLEMENTING THE DIET

In most cases, if you are feeding a professional-quality diet that is complete and well balanced, supplementing is not necessary. Remember, your Boston's system is complex, and to run efficiently it must receive the proper amounts of nutrients in a balanced ratio. By supplementing your Boston's diet, you may inadvertently upset that intricate balance. When there is too much of one nutrient and too little of another, your Boston's diet is out of balance. Fat-soluble vitamins, for example, are stored in a dog's body, so it is easy to overdose with supplementation, causing nutritional imbalances.

A supplement is anything that is given in addition to a dog's feed. It can include something as simple as adding a splash of vegetable oil, a few pieces of leftover steak or half a cup of chicken broth to increase the palatability of your dog's food. While these tidbits are not likely to upset your Boston's nutritional balances—provided they account for less than ten percent off your dog's caloric intake—too many delicacies can add unnecessary calories, resulting in unwanted weight gain.

Nutraceuticals

On the retail side, canine supplements are a multimillion dollar business. Nutraceuticals are a type of supplement and are often called phytochemicals or functional foods. They

Bostons will gladly accept people food or other tasty tidbits—it's your job to provide them in moderation.

include natural remedies such as vitamins, botanicals, nutrients, and minerals. The Nutraceuticals Institute defines them as "natural, bioactive chemical compounds that have health-promoting, disease-preventing or medicinal properties." All nutraceuticals are supplements, but not all supplements are nutraceuticals.

The most popular canine nutraceuticals are the joint-protective products—glucosamine, chondroitin, and methylsulfonylmethane (MSM)—that are typically prescribed for older dogs and are used to help diminish the symptoms of osteoarthritis—the wear-and-tear type of arthritis. They are also used to reduce injuries to joint surfaces, and to promote the healing of cartilage.

While nutraceuticals are popular alternatives to many of the traditional, synthesized medications, they are not without problems. For starters, they are not subject to FDA regulation, and as a result they are poorly regulated. For example, they might not be properly labeled. Also, there is little scientific evidence about nutraceuticals. What experts know about nutraceuticals and their use in the treatment of dogs is empirical. Simply put, the evidence comes less from clinical trials and more from the anecdotes and testimonials of veterinarians and dog people, such as handlers, breeders, and trainers.

In addition to the popular joint-protective products, there are nutraceuticals that claim to promote strong joints and bones, encourage healthy skin and coats, support healthy hips, enhance digestion, calm nervous dogs, and reduce stress. If there is an ailment—there is a supplement marketed to promote, fix, or cure it.

It is important to note that *alternative* or *herbal* does not mean harmless. Supplements can cause side effects or result in cross-reactions if combined with other supplements or medications. To prevent problems, always consult your veterinarian before using supplements.

PROBLEMS WITH FEEDING & EATING

Obesity

Like people, dogs that carry extra pounds are subject to serious health issues, including diabetes, heart disease, increased blood pressure, and digestive disorders. They have increased surgical risks, decreased immune functions, and are more susceptible to injuries including damage to joints, bones, and ligaments. Bostons with patellar luxation, a condition where the kneecap slips out of place, suffer worse symptoms when they are overweight. As a breed, Bostons are predisposed to breathing difficulties and heat intolerance, both of which are exacerbated by obesity. It's a sad but true fact that overweight and obese Boston Terriers have a diminished quality of life, and they tend to die at a younger age than their physically fit counterparts.

How can you help your Boston fight the battle of the bulge? If your Boston is currently overweight or obese, the first step should be a trip to the veterinarian. Some medical conditions, such as hypothyroidism and Cushing's disease, can contribute to weight gain, but those cases represent a very small portion of overweight dogs, perhaps less than five percent, according to experts. Some medications, such as prednisone and phenobarbital, can influence a dog's metabolism and appetite. A veterinarian can examine your Boston to assess his overall health and medical condition, and can advise you on sensible and healthy ways to reduce your Boston's weight.

It is easier to keep the weight off than it is to take it off. If your Boston is not overweight, the most thoughtful and compassionate thing you can do is help prevent him from

Weight gain is a problem for smaller, less active dogs like Boston Terriers, who always love to eat.

Foods to Die For

You might be a chocoholic, but your Boston should not be. Dogs have different metabolisms, and some human foods (and nonfood items) can cause serious health problems ranging from a mild upset stomach to death. Dogs are not the best judges when it comes to what is and is not good for them. After all, some will gleefully eat poop, rocks, and dirt, if you let them. The list below is a sampling of some of the most common foods that can cause your Boston serious health problems if ingested. It is in your dog's best interest to keep him from accessing these items. If you suspect your Boston Terrier has ingested a toxic substance, do not delay and seek veterinary attention immediately.

- Alcoholic beverages can cause intoxication, coma, and, in some instances, death.
- Cooked bones from fish, poultry, or other meat sources can cause obstruction or laceration of the digestive system.
- Cat food, while not fatal, is high in protein and fat and particularly appetizing for enterprising Bostons. Too much can cause intestinal upset and unnecessary weight gain.
- Chocolate, while delicious to people, can be deadly for dogs. It can increase a dog's heart rate and breathing, resulting in serious illness and death.
- Grapes and raisins contain an unknown toxin that can damage your Boston's kidneys.
- Macadamia nuts contain an unknown toxin that can affect your Boston's digestive and nervous systems and muscles. A double dose of trouble is chocolate-covered macadamia nuts.
- Mushrooms can contain toxins that vary depending on the species. They affect multiple systems resulting in shock and death. They grow in the wild—and your backyard. Closely supervise your dog to prevent ingestion.
- Onions and garlic contain sulfoxides and disulfides, which can be toxic to dogs. They can damage red blood cells, causing anemia.
- Tobacco contains nicotine and can cause an increased heartbeat, collapse, coma, and death.

gaining extra pounds. Bostons that are overweight as young dogs are at a greater risk to remain overweight as adult dogs.

Feeding the Right Food

To keep your Boston fit and trim, you need to choose the food that best suits your dog's activity level and life stage. Overweight and underweight dogs, as well as puppies, athletic, and geriatric dogs, have different nutritional and caloric requirements. Puppies require specially formulated diets. An older, less active Boston will generally need fewer calories than a young, energetic Boston, and an overweight Boston may require a special reduced calorie. When in doubt, always seek veterinary assistance in choosing the food that best suits your Boston.

Remember, most dog food manufacturers are overly generous with their guidelines, so by feeding the amount recommended by manufacturers, you may be inadvertently overfeeding your Boston. When in doubt about the correct amount to feed, consult your veterinarian or a knowledgeable Boston Terrier breeder.

Feeding Table Scraps

If your Boston Terrier is willing to bargain with the devil in exchange for a tasty tidbit from the table, you will need to grow a thick skin and ignore his woeful and pleading stare. Table scraps are one of the worst offenders when it comes to sabotaging your dog's weight-maintenance program. A tasty tidbit of steak here, a nibble of chicken there, a potato skin, a French fry or two—what's the harm, right? It is better for table scraps to go to *waste* than your Boston's *waist*. If you cannot resist feeding a tidbit of leftover steak or chicken, put it in the refrigerator and feed it at a later time as a training treat. Feeding from the table also encourages begging, which is a difficult habit to break.

IS MY BOSTON OVERWEIGHT?

A nutritious, well-balanced diet is a sure way to keep your Boston fit, lean, and happy, and can increase his lifespan by nearly two years! It's also one of the most kindhearted gifts you can give your dog. Bostons have a short coat, so viewing their physique is relatively easy. His weight can range from ideal to slightly overweight to downright obese—or somewhere in between. To be sure your Boston is not packing extra pounds, follow these simple guidelines for assessing your Boston's weight:

- Ideally, you should be able to feel your Boston's ribs, and they should have minimal fat covering them. When viewed from the side, his abdominal tuck—the underline of his body where his belly appears to draw up toward his hind end—should be evident. When standing over your Boston and viewing him from above, his waist—the section behind his ribs—should be prominent.
- On a Boston that is a few pounds overweight, you can still feel his ribs, but they have a slight excess of fat covering them. His waist, when viewed from above, is visible, but not nearly as prominent as with a lean Boston. His abdominal tuck is still evident.
- On a Boston that is more than a few pounds overweight, you will have difficulty feeling his ribs. There will be a thick or heavy layer of fat covering them. His waist, when viewed from above, is barely visible. His abdominal tuck may still be present.

If your Boston is well trained, you can put him on a down-stay while you eat, and then verbally praise him for being a good boy. A word of caution: It is difficult, if not impossible, for some dogs, especially young dogs, to maintain their composure when in the presence of food. It is better to restrict his access to the dinner table than to continually tell him to stop begging.

Puppies learn quickly that cookie jars are sources of yummy treats!

- On a very overweight Boston you can't feel his ribs because of the heavy layer of fat covering them. His back and hip region will have fat deposits, and his waist is nonexistent. His abdominal tuck is gone, and his belly will most likely appear distended.
- Forget about feeling the ribs on an obese Boston, because they are buried under heavy layers of fat. He has no waist or abdominal tuck. He may also have fat deposits on his spine, chest, shoulders, neck, and legs.

Begging

If you do not want your Boston begging for food, you should discourage the behavior from day one. Some owners are under the mistaken impression that treating their Boston to tasty tidbits of people food will make him love them more. Not so! A Boston that is rewarded for begging quickly learns to manipulate you. It is a short leap from sad and sympathetic beggar to seasoned con artist. Preventing begging behaviors is easy if you make it a rule from day one that no one—this includes kids, spouses, in-laws, and visitors—feed the dog from the table or at any other time while they are eating.

With eyes that plead for sharing food, it's often difficult to resist, but resist you must for the health of your Boston and your sanity.

Puppies should be kept away from the table while you eat so they are not inadvertently rewarded by dropped food. An alternative is to use a baby gate to keep your Boston corralled in another room and away from where you are eating, where he will be able to see you while you eat and also get used to waiting patiently.

Remember, any table scraps or bits and pieces of food, even when used as training treats, should be included in your dog's daily caloric count. Otherwise, your Boston is likely to put on a few extra pounds.

Take Food Nicely, or "Gentle"

Some puppies seem to naturally take food nicely without trying to trim your cuticles or chew your fingers. Other pup-

Teaching "Gentle"

A good technique to discourage snapping or snatching at food is to keep your hand still. This is easier said than done because instinctively your first reaction is to pull your hand away to avoid getting nipped. If you can keep your hand still as your puppy approaches, he will be less inclined to snap. Before giving him a treat, remind him "Gentle," or "Easy!" so he learns to be gentler with his teeth. At first, he may be clumsy and will probably try to chew at your fingers. Remind him, "Gentle!" When he shows restraint and makes an effort to take the food without using his teeth, let him have the treat and praise him. In the future, before giving him a treat remind him, "Gentle."

pies need to be taught early on not to bite the hand that feeds them—literally! It is in your Boston's best interest to nip this behavior in the bud right away (so to speak) as, left unchecked, it can get downright nasty. Keep in mind that you may inadvertently be teaching your puppy to snatch at food if you are pulling your hand away as he starts to take the food.

If your Boston has already developed the annoying and painful habit of snapping at or snatching food, try this approach: Hold a tasty tidbit of food in the palm of your hand and then fold your hand so you make a fist. Offer him the back of your hand. He will be able to smell the treat, but your fingers will not be exposed or vulnerable. Most likely, he will sniff your hand trying to expose the treat. If he is gentle, open your hand and present the treat in the palm of your hand. He will be able to take the treat without nipping your fingers. As he does so, praise him warmly. Eventually, he will learn to wait until you have opened your hand before he gets a treat.

GROOMING
5
YOUR BOSTON TERRIER

Grooming your Boston Terrier on a regular basis not only keeps his coat in tip-top condition, but also allows you to check his entire body for lumps, bumps, cuts, rashes, dry skin, fleas, ticks, and the like. You can check his feet for cuts, torn pads, or broken nails, and examine his mouth for tartar, damaged teeth, or discolored gums. Regular grooming will improve your Boston's appearance, and since most dogs love to be groomed, this is a great way to spend quality time with your dog while simultaneously building a strong and mutually trusting human/canine relationship.

For the household companion, as opposed to the competitive show dog, grooming is a relatively simple process as long as it is done regularly, and the dog views it as a positive and enjoyable experience.

If you've got a Boston puppy, it's a good idea to start good grooming practices right away. Just because Boston Terriers have a short coat doesn't mean the breed needs no grooming. If your puppy came from a reputable breeder, he's probably used to being handled and gently stroked. He's probably had at least one bath and may already be accustomed to and tolerate being brushed and examined. A puppy that is exposed to positive and delightful grooming experiences will grow into an adult dog that takes pleasure in the regular routine. Few things are as frustrating as trying to wrestle down a Boston Terrier who hates to be groomed.

GETTING YOUR BOSTON USED TO GROOMING

If grooming is new to your Boston, don't despair. Like anything else, it is best to start slow and progress at a rate that is suitable for the age and mental maturity of your dog.

If you have a grooming table, begin by teaching your Boston to stand on the table. Otherwise, any surface such as a bench, crate top, kitchen table, or countertop, covered with a nonskid, nonslip surface is sufficient. Sitting or kneeling on the floor with your Boston works in a pinch, too. In addition, it is prudent to have all of the grooming tools out and within easy reach *before* you start grooming. You never want to turn your back or leave your Boston on the table unattended. A Boston can easily be injured should he fall or jump.

Puppies have limited attention spans, so don't expect your Boston to stand still for extended periods of time. All you want is for him to stand still for a few seconds while you praise him. Harsh handling during these learning stages will only build resentment toward this necessary task.

Progress to the point where your puppy will accept having his body stroked with your hand, then gently, slowly, and calmly brush him all over. In the beginning, your Boston may be frightened, nervous, or unsure. Patience and kind handling will help to build his confidence and teach him to accept and enjoy brushing.

A common problem is for owners to make grooming a game, or to allow the dog to make it a game. Grooming should definitely be a positive and pleasant experience, but a dog that views grooming as a game is likely to become overstimulated and nip or bite at the hand that grooms him. It's best to curtail that behavior right away, as it can become an established behavior that is difficult to break.

REGULAR GROOMING CARE

Brushing

Breeders, owners, and professional groomers have their own routine, established habits, idiosyncrasies, and favorite products and equipment when it comes to grooming. No

Having a grooming table and all your supplies ready makes the job infinitely easier.

doubt, you too will establish your personal preferences as you develop your own grooming knowledge. For most Bostons, a soft bristle brush or grooming glove is usually sufficient for whisking away pieces of debris, dust, dirt, and dead hair. Despite their short coats, Boston Terriers still shed, which is a natural process where strands of hair die, fall out (shed), and are replaced by new hairs. Brushing helps to whisk away these dead hairs, promote and distribute natural oils, and bring out the shine and natural luster in a dog's coat.

Some breeders and groomers recommend starting at the dog's head, brushing in one long stroke toward the tail and then down the sides and legs. Others prefer starting at the feet and working upward. Still others recommend hand-rubbing the hair against the direction of growth to loosen dirt and debris, and then drying with the grain of the coat. Regardless of which method you choose, once-a-week brushings are sufficient, but a five-minute once-over each day with a soft brush or glove is ideal and will help to maintain a Boston's coat and keep it looking velvety.

A thorough grooming gives you the chance to inspect your dog all over, noting coat condition, checking for bumps, and much more.

As you brush, pay particular attention to the condition of his coat. A Boston's coat is a reflection of his health. A glossy, healthy coat begins on the inside with proper nutrition. Is your Boston's coat sleek and glossy? Velvety? Or is it dull, brittle, and lackluster? Is his skin dry and flaky? Does it have a bad smell or that unmistakable *doggie* odor? Do you see bare spots where hair is missing? Any of these conditions could be a sign of inadequate grooming, illness (including allergies), parasitic infestation, or an inadequate diet. When in doubt, a veterinarian can diagnosis the problem and recommend suitable treatments.

Nail Trimming

Owners are often reluctant to trim their dogs' nails for fear of hurting the dog or making him bleed. Even the most experienced groomers have, on occasion, clipped a dog's nail too short, cut the "quick," and caused some bleeding. However, learning how to do it properly, using the correct equipment, and having a dog that accepts having his feet

While some dogs can and will tolerate having their nails trimmed, others prefer for their owners to use a nail grinder. Whichever you choose, be sure to keep your dog's nails short.

handled will go a long way in reducing the odds of inadvertently nipping the quick. In the beginning, you may need someone to help hold your dog, but once you get used to it, trimming your Boston's nails is no more difficult than trimming your own. When in doubt, ask a veterinarian, groomer, or breeder to show you how to do it properly. Or have a professional trim them regularly, which can mean every week or two depending on the dog.

Few Bostons, especially those that spend the majority of their time indoors or on grass when outdoors, will wear down their nails naturally. If your dog's nails make the unmistakable *click, click, click* as he walks on hardwood, tile, or vinyl floors, his nails are too long. Ideally, a dog's nails should not touch the ground. This allows a dog to stand squarely and compactly on the pads of his feet. Nails that are too long put undue stress on the paw by forcing the weight onto the back of the pad. Nails that are too long can be broken, torn off, or snagged, and can scratch furniture, hardwood floors, and skin. Most important, torn or broken nails can cause a Boston a great deal of pain and discomfort, and may become infected. Veterinary attention may be necessary in order to remove the nail completely.

As with other aspects of grooming, it is best to introduce your Boston to the practice of nail care at a young age. With any luck, the breeder will have started snipping small pieces of nail as part of the socialization process and to build the puppy's confidence and teach him to accept having his feet handled. If you choose to clip the nails yourself, it is highly advisable to invest in a good-quality nail clipper designed specifically for dogs. The cost is minimal, about $12 to $15. In the beginning, depending on the puppy's level of cooperation, you may want to simply touch the nail clipper to the puppy's nail and then offer plenty of praise. Progress to clipping tiny bits of nail and then trimming off the remaining dead nail in small bits—avoiding the nail quick.

When a Boston has black nails it can be difficult to differentiate between the quick and the nail. The quick is a blood vessel that travels approximately three-quarters of the way through the nail. As the nail grows, so too does the quick. For that reason, it's better to get in the habit of trimming small bits of nail on a regular basis rather than waiting for the nails to get too long. If accidentally nicked, the quick can bleed profusely and can be difficult to stop. There are a number of

Dogs that are used to being gently handled all over, which starts as a baby, are more cooperative when it comes to grooming.

blood-clotting products available through retail stores, such as powdered alum, styptic powder, or styptic pencil. It is always a good idea to have one of these products in your doggie first-aid kit anytime you plan to be trimming nails.

If you accidentally cut the quick, your Boston will most certainly be a bit tentative or nervous and will not want you to continue. However, it's important that you resist babying or coddling him. It's difficult not to bundle him in your arms and kiss and fuss over him, but this will only feed into his fear and nervousness. Proceeding with caution, clip one more nail, then stop the procedure and lavish him with praise and kisses, then brush a bit more, then clip another nail, then more kisses, more brushing, more clipping, and so forth until the nails are completed.

Some owners prefer to file the dog's nails with a hand file or an electric or battery-operated file. Some use a combination of both clippers and files. Electric or battery-operated files are not without hazards, however. They have an abrasive tip—similar to sandpaper—that spins at a high speed. If used incorrectly, an owner can apply too much pressure or file too close to the quick, causing a dog a good deal of discomfort. These types of instruments make whirling noises and the vibration on the dog's nails can take some getting used to. If started at a young age, many Bostons will accept it as part of the routine grooming process.

If your Boston has dewclaws, be sure not to overlook them in the trimming process. Dewclaws are the fifth digit on the inside of the front legs, usually an inch or so above the feet. If left unattended, they can curl around and grow into the soft tissue, not unlike an ingrown toenail on a human. Some breeders have the dewclaws removed, so your Boston may or may not have them.

A dog whose nails are properly trimmed stands correctly and can't be heard clicking across hard floors.

The Hair on Your Boston's Paws

Bostons have hair that grows between the pads of their feet. When the hair is allowed to get too long, it grows over the pads and can make walking on some surfaces difficult because the dog can't get enough traction. No doubt, it's equally uncomfortable for a Boston to be walking with a wad of hair balled up under his foot. If necessary, use blunt-tipped safety scissor to trim the excess hair on the bottom of his feet. Be careful not to pinch or cut his paw while trimming.

EAR CARE

The Boston Terrier has naturally erect ears that are less vulnerable to infection than the flopped or folded ears of some other breeds. However, that doesn't mean the breed is immune to ear problems. You should examine your Boston's ears regularly for wax, ear mites, and other irritations. If your Boston walks or plays in pastures, fields, or areas with heavy underbrush, you'll want to check them frequently for stickers, burrs, and other foreign matter.

To remove dirt and debris, use an ear-cleaning product specifically designed for dogs. Place a few drops of cleaner into the dog's ear canal and then gently massage the base of the ear for about 20 seconds or so. This helps to soften and loosen the

The key to preventing ear problems is to keep the ears clean.

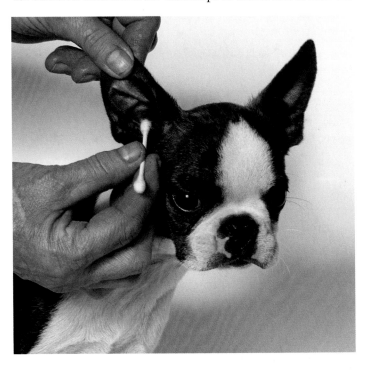

Never stick a cotton swab into the ear canal, as you could cause damage to the eardrum.

debris. At this point, it's okay to let your dog have a good head shake to eject the cleaning solution and debris from the ear canal. Next, apply some ear-cleaning solution onto a clean cotton or gauze pad. Gently wipe the inside ear leather (ear flap), and the part of the ear canal that you can see.

Remember the old adage, "Never stick anything smaller than your elbow in your ear"? The same concept applies to dogs. Never stick cotton swabs or pointed objects into the ear canal because this tends to pack the debris rather than remove it. More important, you risk injuring your dog's eardrum should you probe too deeply.

EYE CARE

A Boston's eyes can be cleaned by saturating a gauze pad with warm water, and then starting at the inside corner of the eye, gently wipe out toward the outside corner of the eye. If you notice any redness, swelling, discoloration, or discharge, these may be signs of an infection. If you suspect something is wrong, do not hesitate to call your veterinarian.

The Boston's large, expressive eyes are one of his finest features. Keep them looking good by gently cleaning around them.

ANAL GLANDS

Dogs have anal glands on each side of the anus. When viewing a dog from behind, they are located at approximately the four and eight o'clock positions. The glands are usually emptied naturally with bowel movements. However, it is not uncommon for them to become impacted (clogged), infected, or abscessed. When the glands become full and uncomfortable, a Boston may scoot along the floor, or lick the anal area excessively. Abscessed or infected glands can be very painful, and a dog may be hesitant to allow you to touch around the area.

When glands become clogged, they must be *expressed*, or emptied, by applying pressure to the glands. There are internal and external pressures, and while some owners have learned to do it themselves, many prefer to leave it to a veterinarian or qualified groomer.

Abscessed anal glands require veterinary attention, as do some impacted or clogged glands.

BATHING YOUR BOSTON

How often your Boston requires bathing will depend on

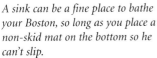

A sink can be a fine place to bathe your Boston, so long as you place a non-skid mat on the bottom so he can't slip.

where you live, how much time he spends outside, and how dirty he gets. If he is your constant companion on walks, jogs, hikes, and trips to the barn or pasture, he may require bathing on a regular basis, say, every few weeks or so. If he spends a great deal of time indoors, he may require bathing once every three or four months. There is no exact formula for how often your Boston needs bathing. You'll need to be the judge.

The Boston's small size makes him an ideal breed for bathing in the kitchen sink, utility sink, or bathtub. A rubber mat on the bottom of the sink or tub will provide secure footing and prevent him from slipping. A cotton ball placed in each ear will keep the water out. Unless your dog has a specific skin condition, such as dry, flaky, itchy skin, choose a mild shampoo designed specifically for dogs. Some shampoos contain harsh detergents that can dry the skin and damage the coat by stripping it of natural oils. There are many shampoo and conditioning products from all-purpose to medicating to herbal to color enhancing, so don't be shy about asking for help when choosing shampoos and conditioners.

Saturate your Boston with warm water, apply a dab of shampoo to the palm of your hand, suds it up, and scrub away! Work the shampoo into the coat with your fingers or a rubber massage tool designed specifically for dogs. Scrub from head to toe, being careful to avoid the eye area. To clean around a Boston's sensitive eyes, wipe the area with a damp cloth. You can also use a small dab of tearless shampoo to gently wash around the head and eye area. Even though it's tearless, it is best to avoid getting any in your dog's eyes. Rinse his entire body thoroughly with warm water. The rinsing is the most important part.

Residual shampoo can irritate the skin, as well as leave a dull film on the coat. If necessary, shampoo and rinse again to be sure your Boston is squeaky clean! If you are using a coat conditioner or skin moisturizer, be sure to follow directions carefully. If possible, let your Boston shake off any extra water, then towel dry him thoroughly.

Throughout the entire bath and until he is completely dry again, protect him from any drafts. While blow-drying isn't normally necessary, it is an option if you think your Boston runs the risk of getting chilled. When using a hair dryer, hold the dryer at least six to eight inches away from the coat, keep the dryer in motion, and use a low or cool heat setting to avoid damaging the coat or burning your Boston's skin.

DENTAL CARE

Just as you take good care of your teeth, it is essential that you take good care of your Boston's teeth. Bostons are prone to overcrowding in their mouths, which makes a home-care dental routine essential. The importance of high-quality dental hygiene cannot be understated. If left unattended, your Boston can develop periodontal disease, a progressive disorder that can, in advanced cases, lead to decayed gums, infection, and liver, kidney, and heart damage.

Dental problems in dogs begin the same way they do in humans—with plaque. Plaque is a colorless film and is the major culprit in periodontal disease. Plaque begins with the accumulation of food particles and bacteria along the gum line. Germs present in plaque attack the gums, bone, and ligaments that support the teeth, and routine home care can help remove this plaque. However, when left untreated, minerals and saliva combine with the plaque and harden into a substance called tartar. As the tartar accumulates, it starts irritating your dog's gums,

causing an inflamed condition called *gingivitis* that is easily identified by the yellowish-brown crust on the teeth and the reddening of gums next to the teeth. In the early stages, periodontal disease is generally reversible, provided your Boston starts receiving sufficient, routine oral hygiene. Otherwise, the process continues to erode the gums and tissues that support the teeth, which can lead to pain and tooth loss. As bad as that sounds, it can get worse.

If the tartar is not removed, the cycle continues to repeat itself, encouraging even more bacterial growth. The tartar builds up under the gums causing the gums to separate from the teeth, causing even larger pockets where more debris can collect. At this stage, your Boston's teeth no doubt have quite an accumulation of highly visible, crusty, yellowish-brown tartar. Brushing your Boston's teeth on a regular basis will remove plaque, but not tartar. If your Boston already has a tartar buildup, he'll need to see a veterinarian to have it removed and his teeth polished.

In most advanced stages, damage from the periodontal disease is considered irreversible because bacterial infection has been busy destroying your Boston's gums, teeth, and bones. In addition, bacteria can also enter the bloodstream, causing secondary infections that can damage your dog's heart, liver, and kidneys.

A good dental hygiene program includes an annual veterinary exam. A veterinarian will check for potential problems, such as plaque and tartar buildup, gingivitis, periodontal disease, and fractured or abscessed teeth. If necessary, a veterinarian may recommend professional dental cleaning, also known as prophylaxis or prophy. While anesthetized, a dog's mouth is flushed with a solution to kill bacteria, the teeth are cleaned to remove any tartar, polished, inspected, and flushed again with an antibacterial solution. Fractured teeth may require reconstructive surgery not unlike people receive, such as root canals and crowns.

Brushing Your Dog's Teeth

The best way to prevent periodontal disease is to keep your Boston's teeth clean. The process is relatively simple and requires nothing more than a small number of fairly inexpensive supplies and few minutes of your time.

You will need either a child-size soft bristle toothbrush, a

pet toothbrush, gauze for wrapping around a finger, or a finger toothbrush, which, as the name suggests, simply slides over your finger, and some toothpaste designed specifically for dogs. A word of caution: Do not use human toothpaste. It is not designed for dogs and can upset your dog's stomach. Most canine toothpastes are formulated with poultry or malt flavored enhancers for easier acceptance.

As with other aspects of grooming, it is much easier to begin introducing oral hygiene to a puppy, but it's never too late to begin. You will need to start slowly and progress at a pace suitable for your Boston Terrier. Most dogs, be they young or old, will no doubt take issue with a toothbrush being jammed into their mouth, so start by using your fin-

How Often to Brush?

Ideally, you should strive to brush your Boston's teeth on a daily basis, just like you do with your own teeth. Like anything else, the hardest part is getting started. However, once you accustom your Boston to having his teeth brushed,, you can incorporate it into your daily schedule. For instance, you might try incorporating it into your nightly routine, such as before you go to bed. You can make a production of it so your dog views it as a fun game you do together. Ask him in a happy, excited voice, "Do you want to brush your teeth?" When you're done, praise him. If brushing every day seems an impossible task, try to brush your dog's teeth every other day or at least once a week.

ger to gently massage his gums. Put a small dab of doggie toothpaste on your index finger and let your dog lick it, then praise him. Apply another dab on your finger, gently lift up his outer lips, and massage his gums.

Ideally, it is best to massage in a circular motion, but sometimes you need to be satisfied with simply getting your finger in your dog's mouth. Try to massage both top and bottom, and the front gums, too. If he's a puppy, watch out for those sharp baby teeth, and remember to keep a positive attitude, praising your Boston and reassuring him throughout the process. It is also helpful if you try to avoid wrestling with your dog or restraining him too tightly. This will only hamper the process and make him resistant to this necessary routine.

While Bostons aren't known for their toothy grins, regular dental care can assure you that all is well behind those jowls.

Once your dog is comfortable with this process, try using a toothbrush, finger toothbrush, or a gauze pad wrapped around your finger. Let your dog lick some toothpaste off the toothbrush or gauze pad and, again, praise him. This will help accustom him to the texture of the brush or gauze while building his confidence.

You are now ready to begin brushing. As before, lift the outer lips and expose the teeth. Most owners find it easiest to start with the canine teeth—the large ones in the front of the mouth. They are the easiest to reach, and you should be able to brush them with little interference or objection from your dog. Once your dog is accustomed to you brushing a few teeth, progress to a few more, then a few more until you've brushed all 42 teeth (or 28 teeth if you have a puppy).

CHEW TOYS FOR DENTAL HYGIENE

You can also try using any number of chew/dental toys available for dogs that help to remove plaque. Select products that are right for the chewing style of your Boston, and that are made to last. Nylabones are recommended by veterinarians, breeders, and trainers. Learn more about them at www.nylabone.com. Toys should not replace brushing, but they will help to remove some of the plaque, exercise your Boston's jaw, and satisfy his need to chew. Be sure to keep an eye on the toys and toss them when they get too small and become possible choking hazards. Be sure to avoid toys and bones that are hard enough to crack or break an aggressive chewer's teeth.

Dogs have four types of teeth and each has a different function:
- Incisors are used for cutting and nibbling food.
- Canines are used for holding and tearing food.
- Premolars are used for cutting, holding, and shearing food.
- Molars are for grinding food.

A supply of chew toys designed to promote dental health will also benefit your Boston.

TRAINING AND BEHAVIOR

OF YOUR BOSTON TERRIER

Owning and training a Boston Terrier can be simultaneously exhilarating and exhausting. Some days, it can seem remarkably like the joys and frustrations of raising toddlers and teenagers. The good news is that teaching basic obedience commands is a relatively simple process. Most of the problems you will encounter are entirely predictable, and armed with a good game plan and a bit of knowledge many problems are entirely preventable. At the very least, you can prevent them from escalating into major stumbling blocks.

The object of teaching basic obedience skills is to provide your Boston with a set of commands he understands, thereby making your life and his more enjoyable. Having to shout multiple commands at your dog, or having to physically restrain him, makes dog ownership exhausting and frustrating. A Boston Terrier—even a very small one—that does not have a solid foundation of obedience skills or canine manners can quickly grow into an unruly hooligan. A Boston that is taught to respond reliably and quickly to basic commands is much easier and enjoyable to live with. No doubt, his life is more pleasurable because as a well-behaved dog, he is more likely to be incorporated into the family environment rather than relegated to the isolation of the backyard.

TYPES OF TRAINING

There are many wonderful methods for training puppies and adult dogs. The hardest part is choosing from the enormous variety of training methods and trainers. What works, what doesn't? Who's right, who's wrong? In today's canine-friendly environment, it seems there are as many trainers and training methods as there are breeds of dogs. There's positive and negative motivation, food training, play training, toy training, and clicker training. Throw in the endless variety of paraphernalia employed—from electronic gizmos to metallic gadgetry—and the entire process can seem more complicated than computer science.

The good news is that raising and training a Boston Terrier is not terribly difficult and is well within the capabilities of most dog owners who set their mind to it. It does, however, require time, insight, dedication, and the ability to view setbacks with a sense of humor. While most Bostons have a willingness and desire to please, they can also have their own agenda when it comes to training, so an endless reserve of patience is a virtue. A key ingredient to successful dog

Boston Terriers who have received some training are easier and more enjoyable to live with.

training is having a clear picture of what you want to accomplish and a well-thought-out game plan, which includes regular training, socialization, and interaction with your puppy both at home and in public. Additionally, it helps if you start right away—preferably, as soon as your Boston starts living with you.

Years ago, the accepted methodology of dog training was that a puppy had to be at least six months old before you began teaching basic obedience skills. That concept has since been debunked and modern-day breeders, trainers, and animal behaviorists now recognize the important benefits of training as early as five weeks of age. Additionally, trainers from the past often employed the standard *pop and jerk* type training that involved a choke chain, force, and a total domination of the dog. While that method usually produced desired results, it often came at a price that included stifling

Today, trainers advise owners to work with their dogs using positive rather than punitive training methods.

a dog's unique personality, as well as his willingness and desire to please. Many of those methods produced dogs that obeyed commands out of fear rather than a desire to please their owners.

Today's top trainers had the foresight and willingness to change by recognizing the importance of allowing dogs and handlers to be themselves rather than imposing the same training method regardless of temperament. While you can still find trainers that adhere to the ideology of force and domination as a means of training, most trainers today employ gentler training methods that include praise, positive motivation, and positive reinforcement.

The concept behind positive motivation/reinforcement is that when a behavior has favorable consequences, the probability of that behavior being repeated is increased. A dog, for example, learns to repeat a behavior, such as sit, down, or come, in order to receive a reward. The reward can be a combination of verbal or physical praise coupled with a tasty tidbit of food or his favorite toy.

Formal Versus Informal Training

Training should be fun for both you and your dog. Otherwise, what's the point? The goal is to teach your dog to cheerfully and eagerly respond to a variety of commands both on and off leash and under a range of circumstances, such as in your yard, at the park, and even when he is playing with his canine buddies. Where owners often run afoul with their dog's training is by getting caught up in the formal versus informal training debate. The only real difference between formal and informal training is the degree of precision. If you are interested in competitive obedience with your Boston, then you will need to ask for more precision as your dog matures. Formal training, however, does not mean all work and no play. It should be equally as fun as informal training.

KEEP IT FUN!

Regardless of whether you call it formal or informal training, you can maximize your dog's training by avoiding techniques that are repetitive, predictable, and boring for your dog. Bostons are quick, bright, active, and always ready for a game, so use your imagination and be creative. Come up with fun training techniques and games that stimulate your Boston's mind and increase his desire to learn.

Dogs are naturally curious and love to explore and test their boundaries. Therefore, it is best to begin your dog's training in a familiar environment that has a limited number of distractions, such as your house or yard. This is especially helpful if you are training a young puppy.

Puppies have very limited attentions spans and are easily distracted by kids playing, toys lying around, birds flying overhead, a bug on the ground, cows mooing, and so forth. It is unreasonable to expect a young puppy to ignore all the distractions and focus entirely on you. "It's a bit like taking a child to Disneyland for the first time and expecting it to learn logarithms," says English dog trainer Annette Conn, and author of the book, *It's a Dog's Life.*

FINDING A TRAINER

If your Boston Terrier is between two and five months of age, a puppy kindergarten class is an ideal environment for exposing and socializing him to everything he will encounter in his adult life, such as other dogs, kids, stairways, strange noises and smells, trash cans, women in floppy hats, and so forth. Puppy classes will help your Boston continue to expand on his knowledge of canine communication and social skills that he learned from his canine mother and while interacting with his littermates. As he grows and matures, he will learn to communicate and interact with other dogs in a low-risk and stress-free environment.

Puppy classes should not be a free-for-all where puppies play on their own while their owners socialize on the sidelines. A well-structured puppy class will include teaching basic obedience skills including enjoyable puppy recall games, sit, down, and name recognition. You will learn how to read canine body language, how to train your puppy, and how to recognize problems early on before they become annoying, ingrained habits that are difficult to break.

Remember while you're training your dog to make it an enjoyable experience for both of you. Offer plenty of praise, and quit while you're ahead.

To find the right puppy class for you and your Boston:

- Ask your veterinarian, breeder, dog groomer, or dog-owning friends for referrals. Word of mouth is a great tool for uncovering talented and knowledgeable trainers, while avoiding problem ones.
- Contact professional organizations that certify or recommend trainers, such as the Association of Pet Dog Trainers or National Association of Dog Obedience Instructors.
- Attend the classes of several trainers to observe their personalities, training techniques, and facilities.
- Look for trainers who focus on rewarding what your puppy does right rather than punishing what he does wrong.
- Does the trainer recognize that puppies are individuals? Are the same training methods imposed on all the puppies regardless of their mental maturity?
- Puppies learn best in low-risk, stress-free environments. Look for classes that are structured, run smoothly, yet still emphasize fun.
- Do the facilities provide a safe learning environment for you and your puppy? Are they well lit with matted floors and no more than eight to ten puppies per class?
- Are the puppies separated—small puppies from large, young puppies from juniors, the rambunctious from the shy?
- Trust your instincts. Your puppy's safety and well-being are most important. If you feel uncomfortable about the facility or trainer, find another puppy class.

BASIC TRAINING

The first step in teaching any exercise is to have a clear picture in your mind of what you want to teach. If you are teaching your Boston to *sit,* have a clear picture in your mind of what a *sit* looks like. This may seem simple, if not downright silly, but if you cannot visualize it in your mind, how can you teach it and, more important, how can your dog learn it? Many owners have different ideas of what represents a *sit* or a *down* or even a *come* command. Also, some owners are happy if their dog *comes* on the eight or ninth command, while others want their Boston to *come* the first time he's called.

The Sit

Teaching the Sit command is relatively simple and the guidelines are the same whether you are teaching a young puppy or an adult dog.

1. Begin with your puppy on leash. This is especially helpful if your dog, like most puppies, has his own agenda, tends to wander off, or is easily distracted.
2. Start with your leash in one hand, a tasty tidbit in the other hand, and your puppy standing in front of you. (Hold the tidbit firmly between your thumb and index finger so your dog cannot get it until he is in the correct position.)
3. Show your puppy the tidbit by holding it close to and slightly above his nose. As your puppy raises his nose to take the food, slowly move the cookie in a slightly upward and backward direction toward his tail, keeping the cookie directly above his nose. (If your puppy jumps up or brings his front feet off the ground, the cookie is too high. If he walks

A food treat held just over your Boston's head will cause him to sit in order to follow it with his nose. When his rear hits the floor, reward!

backwards, the cookie is too far back or too low.)

4. At this point, your puppy's hips should automatically sink toward the ground. As they do, give the sit command. While your puppy is sitting, praise him with "Good sit!" and reward him with the tidbit. (Give the sit command as your puppy's rear end hits the ground. Saying it too soon will teach the wrong association.)

Release your puppy with a release word, such as *Free* or *OK*, play with him for a few seconds and repeat the exercise three or four times in succession, three or four times a day.

The Down

Teaching the down command can be a bit more challenging than the sit as it is considered a submissive position for some dogs. If your puppy has an independent personality, this exercise will take a bit more patience and persistence on your part. But don't give up! Puppies learn through repetition and consistency.

Get in the habit of saying the command one time. Avoid repeating yourself: "Sit, Sit, Sit, %#$@! Sit!" If you say it ten times, your Boston will wait until the tenth command to respond. Remember to make sure you give your puppy the release word before you allow him to rise out of the sit position. Doing so will clearly signal to the puppy the end of the exercise. Also, avoid saying "sit down" when you really mean "sit."

1. Begin by kneeling on the floor so you are eye level with your puppy.
2. With your puppy standing in front of you, hold a tasty tidbit of food in one hand; place your other hand in his buckle collar under his chin with your fingertips pointing down.
3. Let your puppy sniff the cookie. Simultaneously, move the cookie toward the floor between his front feet while you apply gentle downward and backward pressure with your hand that is in the collar.
4. When done correctly, your puppy will plant his front feet and fold his body into the down position as he follows the cookie to the ground.
5. When his elbows and stomach are on the ground, give the down command.

With a small dog like the Boston Terrier, you should teach a command while you're kneeling beside him.

6. While your puppy is in the down position, reward him with the cookie and *calmly* praise: "Good down."
7. Release your puppy with a release word, such as *Free* or *OK*, repeat the exercise three or four times in succession, three or four times a day.

Tips for Teaching Down

If your puppy resists your hand in the collar, follow the above instructions, but instead of putting your hand in the collar, apply light pressure with the flat of your hand on your Boston's shoulder blades. Avoid sliding your hand down your puppy's back. This may put pressure on the wrong spot and hurt him. If your puppy resists, avoid getting into a wrestling match with him. Simply stop the exercise and try again later.

Make sure you give your puppy a release word before you allow him to rise out of the down position. Doing so will clearly signal to the dog the end of the exercise. Be careful not to use the command "sit down" when you really mean down, and avoid confusing your dog by using the down command when you really mean off—such as getting off the furniture or not jumping on you.

The Stay

The goal is to teach your dog to stay in a specific position, such as in a sit or down, until you say it is okay to move. It is useful in a variety of situations, such as when you want to answer or open the door without your Boston bolting through it.

Sit-Stay

1. Start with your puppy on a loose leash, sitting beside you.
2. Tell your puppy to sit and to stay. You can include a hand signal by holding the open palm of your hand in front of your puppy's face about two inches from his nose as you say "Stay."
3. Watch your dog closely for the slightest movement that may indicate he is about to stand up or lie down. Try to be proactive in your training by reminding your dog to stay *before* he moves.

Once he has remained in position for a few seconds, praise calmly and warmly with "Good stay" and a tidbit of food. You can include calm, physical praise, such as gentle stroking—but not so enthusiastically that he gets excited and forgets the task at hand.

As soon as you see any movement, repeat your stay command firmly, but not harshly.

If your dog stands up, use your leash to prevent him from

moving away and get him into the sit position again. If he lies down, gently reposition him and remind him to stay.

Reward him with a small food treat first and then release him with an "ok" or "free" command. (If you release your dog first and then reward him, you will teach him the wrong association. He will think he is being rewarding for moving. This can teach a puppy to anticipate the reward, thereby encouraging him to break the stay command.)

As your puppy matures and can remain sitting beside you for two or three minutes without moving, you can progress by giving the stay command and then stepping directly in front of his nose. Gradually begin increasing the distance between you and your puppy.

Once you have a reliable sit-stay in a non-distractive situation, you can begin incorporating mild distractions, such as toys lying nearby on the floor. As your dog becomes reliable with mild distractions, you can begin escalating the distractions. Try training while other people or dogs play nearby. If your dog has a difficult time focusing on the task at hand, perhaps the increase in distractions was too soon or severe.

With consistent training, your Boston will soon be doing reliable sit-stays for you. Good dog!

Tips for Teaching Stay

Many puppies are not emotionally mature enough to cope with this exercise until they are four or five months old. If this is the case with your puppy, don't force the issue. Simply wait until he is older and mentally more mature to understand and cope with the exercise. When first learning this command, five or ten seconds in the stay position is long enough for most dogs. Gradually, over a number of sessions and in five-second increments, increase the time your Boston remains in position.

Do not be in a hurry to move away from your dog or have him hold the position for longer periods. Young puppies have limited attention spans. How fast your Boston progresses with this exercise will depend on his mental maturity. Do not nag, scold, or send him threatening looks during a stay. Dogs that are bullied or intimidated into staying are less reliable in the long run. Dogs learn faster and retain more information when they learn in a stress-free environment. Never leave your dog in a stay position unsupervised, such as outside a store or anywhere he could run off, be hurt, stolen, or lost. Avoid using the stay command when you really mean wait, such as wait in the yard, or wait in the car until I get back.

Down-Stay

To teach the down-stay, begin with your dog in the down position, and tell him to stay.

Then follow the remaining instructions for teaching the sit-stay.

Sit and Accept Praise

The sit and accept praise command differs from the sit-stay command. This exercise is a nice alternative for puppies who are too young for the formal sit-stay exercise. By learning to sit still and accept verbal praise, your puppy learns to control himself and that helps to make teaching the stay command easier when your puppy is older and more mentally mature.

Step One

Begin with your puppy on leash and in a sit. (For this exercise, it's not necessary that he be sitting in heel position.) Talk to your puppy in a calm voice. The key is to talk calmly. If your voice is high-pitched and excited, your puppy will not be able to control himself, and it's highly likely he'll jump up or move about. If your puppy remains sitting while you talk, calmly praise him. If your puppy moves, tell him "No!" in a firm but kind voice. Don't yell or holler "*No!*" This will only scare your puppy, and he'll learn to fear you and the exercise. Gently put your puppy back in the sit position and begin again.

Step Two

Most puppies quickly learn that talking does not mean it is okay for them to get up.

Once your dog can sit reliably while you talk to him, try progressing to the next step.

With your dog on leash and in a sit, inspect his ears. Tell him what you are doing. If your dog remains in a sit, praise him with "Good puppy!" or "Good sit!" Inspect his teeth or pick up one of his feet and count his toes. If your puppy moves, tell him "No" in a firm but kind voice. Gently put your puppy back in the sit and begin again.

As with all of the exercises, progress at a rate that is appropriate for your dog's age and mental capability.

Stand for Examination

In competitive obedience, the *stand for examination* is a formal exercise. A modified version of this exercise—stand for veterinary examination—is helpful when a veterinarian must gently restrain and examine your Boston Terrier. Your veterinarian will greatly appreciate you for teaching this exercise.

It may take a while, but with practice and patience, your Boston will soon master the stand for examination.

Begin with your dog in the standing position. Gently support his stomach by placing your arm under his stomach. The crook of your elbow should be resting under his stomach and the flat of your hand should support the opposite side of his body. While supporting his stomach, gently secure his collar with your free hand. Praise him for standing still.

Remember, puppies have limited attention spans. Your short-term goal is to accustom him to standing still while you gently restrain him. Once your puppy can stand still while you gently restrain and reassure him, begin having family members examine him. They should reward him with tasty tidbits from one hand while running their other hand over his body. Don't forget to verbally praise him, too.

Come When Called

A puppy that views come as a fun game is more likely to develop a reliable response to the command. The goal is to teach your puppy to come to you reliably, willingly, and immediately upon hearing the command, while in a wide range of situations, such as at the park, in the neighbor's yard, at a friend's house, in an emergency, or anytime he gets loose.

"Find me" is an informal game that capitalizes on a dog's natural chase instinct and begins teaching come in a positive, fun, and exciting manner. It's also an excellent game for instilling the come command in young puppies.

1. Start with a pocket full of tasty tidbits.
2. Rev your puppy up by showing him a treat, and then toss the treat down the hallway or across the living room.
3. As your puppy runs for the treat, you run in the opposite direction and hide behind a chair or door as you say his name enthusiastically.
4. When your puppy finds you, make a big fuss: Get on the floor, roll around, and lavish him with kisses and praise.
5. Repeat the game several times throughout the day, but not so many times that your dog becomes bored.

You can also play this game outdoors. Be sure to play in a fenced area to protect your dog from harm or prevent him from running off. When you are outside in your garden or

"Find me" is a great game to play outdoors. You and your dog will have a lot of fun, and it reinforces coming when called.

yard with your dog and he stops to sniff the grass or explore a bug, duck behind a tree or bush, clap your hands, and say his name in an excited tone of voice.

When your dog gets to you, greet him with plenty of hugs, kisses, and praise. It is not necessary for your dog to sit before he gets a treat. If you insist on your puppy sitting first, you will not be rewarding the most important part of the exercise, which is coming to you.

Other Ways to Teach Come

If you do not have access to a fenced area, you can play a similar game by using a long-line or flexible leash.

1. With your dog on leash, wait for his attention to wander.
2. Say his name enthusiastically and give a little flick or pop on the leash (enough to make him turn and look at you but not so much as to frighten or harm him), show him the reward (i.e., the treat), back up quickly as you lure him with the treat, and simultaneously praise him as he moves toward you.
3. If necessary, crouch down or get on the ground so you are eye level with him. When your dog gets to you, reward him with the treat, and shower him with plenty of praise and kisses.
4. Repeat this game two or three times in a row, several times throughout the day.

Tips for Teaching Come

Your dog must always chase you. Avoid making a game of you chasing your dog, and never allow kids to chase your dog. It inadvertently teaches him to run away from you, which creates a myriad of problems down the road. If you want a dog that reliably comes to you when he is called, the come command must always be positive. If your puppy comes to you, you must always, always, always praise him. There is no wiggle room, and there are no exceptions to this rule. Never call your dog with the come command and then correct him for something he did, such as chewing your shoe or urinating on the floor. If you want to correct your dog, go and get him. Do not call him to you. Also, do not call your dog with the come command if you want to give him a bath, administer medications, or anything else he might find unpleasant. Instead, go and get your dog, and then put him in the tub, trim his nails, administer medications, etc.

CRATE TRAINING

A crate is a fantastic training tool when used properly by responsible dog owners. Many owners look upon a crate as cruel or inhumane. Instead, it should be viewed from a dog's perspective. Before dogs became domesticated pets, they tended to seek safe, enclosed areas for security and protection. A crate mimics that safe, enclosed environment. Puppies,

Trick training is easy when you've mastered the principles of dog training, which include keeping training sessions short, fun, and focused.

Seven Tips for Successful Dog Training

1. Puppies and young dogs have limited attention spans. Keep sessions short: train two or three times a day, 5 or 10 minutes per session.
2. Training must always be fun. Fun games maximize your dogs' propensity to learn.
3. Train when your dog is awake and eager to play. Never wake up your dog in order to train.
4. Dogs learn at different rates. Train within your dog's mental and physical capabilities. Never progress at a speed faster than your dog's ability to comprehend.
5. Set achievable goals to keep you and your puppy motivated. Keep training steps small and praise your dog every time he does a tiny step right.
6. Always use a command when you use your dog's name. For example, "Fido, come!" or "Fido, down." If you repeatedly say your dog's name without putting a command with it, it's a form of nagging and eventually your dog will become desensitized to his name.
7. Always end a play/training session on a positive note.

especially very young puppies, tire quickly and need a lot of sleep during the day. A crate placed in a quiet corner of the kitchen or family room will replicate a dog's natural instinct to seek a safe and secure environment. When properly introduced, a crate becomes a safe-zone for your Boston—a quiet place all his own to sleep, eat, and retreat from the poking, prodding fingers of noisy, rambunctious toddlers.

A key to successful puppy rearing is to never put your puppy in a position where he can get himself into trouble. Any puppy left unsupervised will develop bad habits. In record time, your adorable Boston puppy can pee from one end of the house to the other, ransack the trash, and gnaw the leg off your dining room chair. Does the expression, "I just turned my back for a second!" sound familiar? During those short periods when you can't watch your puppy closely, a crate prevents him from getting into mischief.

A crate is one of the safest, most successful and efficient ways to housetrain a young puppy or adult dog. If your Boston has an accident in his crate, the mess is much easier to clean and less damaging than when it's in the middle of your Persian rug.

A crate is also ideal for keeping your Boston safe while traveling. A crated dog will not distract you from your driving responsibilities, teethe on your leather armrests, or eat your cell phone. Many motels and hotels, as well as friends and family, are more receptive to dogs provided they are crate trained. As your Boston grows and matures, the crate will continue to be his den and safe place for eating, sleeping, and retreating from the often chaotic and noisy world of humans.

Introducing the Crate

A crate, like any other training tool, has the potential to be abused. A crate is not intended for 24-hour confinement. Your Boston should live with you and not in his crate. A crate should never be used as a form of punishment. It should provide your Boston with a safe, secure environment. A place your Boston enjoys.

Most puppies quickly learn to love their crate when it is associated with good things, such as feeding, treats, security, and sleep. To maximize the crate-training process:

Make the crate attractive to your puppy by placing an old blanket, towel, or rug and a few of his favorite indestructible chew toys inside the crate. Remember, young puppies love to chew, so choose toys and blankets that are safe and do not present a potential choking hazard.

Leave the crate door open and allow your puppy to explore in and around the crate. If your puppy goes inside the crate, praise him. Reward him with a tasty tidbit while he is in the crate.

If your puppy is reluctant to go inside, encourage him by letting him see you toss a tasty tidbit of food inside the crate, preferably toward the back of the crate. When your puppy

A crate is important and useful for everything from providing your dog with a safe spot of his own, to housetraining, to traveling.

goes inside the crate to retrieve the food, praise him.

Feed your puppy his meals inside the crate, luring him inside with his food bowl. This makes the crate a positive place for your puppy to be.

When your puppy is comfortable being inside the crate and shows no signs of stress, try closing the door for one minute. Do not latch the door. Open the door and praise your puppy for being brave.

As your puppy becomes more comfortable with the crate, you can gradually increase the time that he spends there. Never confine him for longer than one hour at a time—except at night when he is sleeping.

If your puppy begins whining and crying, try to avoid reinforcing the behavior by letting him out or coddling him, such as saying, "What's the matter, honey?" Wait for him to be quiet for a minute or two before opening the door. Of course, you should be certain that he does not need to relieve himself.

If you are working and can't let your puppy out every hour, hire a reliable relative, friend, or neighbor to exercise your puppy during the day. Or, try using a playpen or exercise pen. This will give your puppy room to play, exercise, and relieve himself if necessary.

Housetraining the Crate Way

The object of housetraining is to teach your puppy to relieve himself outdoors and not on your Oriental rug, in the corner of the living room, or from one end of the house to the other. Housetraining is a relatively easy and painless process, yet it often causes owners a great deal of anxiety. Good planning and preparation and your unwavering commitment to the situation will provide your puppy with the best possible start. Crate training, when done properly, helps to quickly and efficiently housetrain a puppy.

Most den animals have an instinctive desire to keep their dens clean. As a result, they instinctively will try not to eliminate in their den. A crate serves as your puppy's den. If you watch a litter of puppies, you will notice around three weeks of age the puppies will instinctively begin moving away from the whelping box in order to relieve themselves. This deep-seated denning instinct and an innate tendency to keep the den clean provide the foundation of housetraining via use of

Housetraining is easier if you keep your dog on a schedule and know the signals for when he has to go, such as sniffing the ground.

a crate. If you take advantage of this instinct, you reduce the chance of accidents. As your puppy matures, you can gradually teach him to hold his bladder for longer periods of time.

To increase your chances of success while minimizing accidents, you will need to provide your puppy with a regular schedule of eating, sleeping, and eliminating. Dogs are creatures of habit, and they will have an easier time adjusting to their new household and a housetraining schedule if you provide some order and routine to their lives.

Understand Your Puppy

The first step in any successful housetraining program is recognizing that young puppies have very little or no bladder control until around five months of age. Puppies mature at different rates, so your puppy's control may develop earlier or later. A seven- or eight-week-old puppy is equivalent to a four- or six-month-old human baby. You would not expect a young baby to control his bladder, and it is unfair to ask your puppy to do so.

Puppies are most active during the day—running, jumping, training, playing, exploring, and being a puppy.

Because of their limited bladder size and lack of control, it goes without saying that they are going to need to relieve themselves many, many times throughout the day. During the night, however, puppies are usually exhausted from their busy day of being a puppy. They are more relaxed, and as a result most puppies can sleep between five and eight hours without having to potty. This varies from puppy to puppy, and in this sense they are not unlike human babies. Some parents get lucky and their babies sleep through the night.

Young puppies, generally under the age of three months, find comfort and security by being close to you. If you leave while your puppy is searching for a spot to potty, he will most likely run after you and forget about the task at hand. If you put him outdoors and leave him to his own devices, it's highly likely he will spend most of his time trying to get back in the house to be with you, and, again, he will have forgotten about the task at hand.

Others are relegated to months of sleeplessness.

For the first several months—until your puppy begins to develop some reliable bladder control—you will need to take him outdoors frequently. If you are 100 percent committed to a regular schedule, your puppy will learn that elimination opportunities occur on a schedule.

As a general guideline to increase your chances of success while minimizing accidents, take your puppy outdoors at the following times:

- First thing in the morning when he wakes up.
- About 15 minutes after drinking water.
- About 30 minutes after eating.
- Immediately after waking from a nap.
- During any excitement, such as when you arrive home, a deliveryman shows up, or guests come to visit.
- At least once every hour during the day.
- Last thing at night.

This guideline is for young puppies. Because puppies are individuals and must be treated as such, you may need to tweak or adjust this schedule to fit your puppy's individual needs. No one said raising a puppy was all fun and no work! Housetraining a puppy is a time-consuming endeavor, but the time invested at this stage will make your life easier in the long run. It may seem unreasonable or unnecessary to take your puppy outside every hour to potty, but taking him out on a regular basis is easier and cheaper and less aggravating than constantly cleaning or replacing carpets. Dogs are either housetrained or they aren't—the fewer mistakes your Boston has as a puppy, the faster he will learn that outside is where he needs to go, and the more reliable he will be as an adult dog.

Gotta Go—Right Now!

First thing each morning when you hear that unmistakable whimper, let your puppy out of his crate and immediately take him outdoors to a designated spot. Do not dawdle or allow yourself to get sidetracked making coffee, checking your e-mail, or fumbling around for a leash—keep one in a convenient spot. A few seemingly insignificant minutes to you is long enough to risk an accident for your puppy. Remember, your puppy has little or no bladder control and has been confined in his crate for six to eight hours. He needs to go immediately.

While you are outside, watch your puppy to make sure he empties his bladder or bowels. It may take a few minutes, so be patient. When your puppy has finished doing his business, calmly praise him. Once you have seen your puppy relieve himself outdoors, you can allow him supervised play indoors. If you take your puppy outdoors and he does not relieve himself, it is important that you put him back in his crate for five or ten minutes and then repeat the aforementioned steps. (If you are not using a crate to housetrain, you will need to keep your puppy where you can watch him for those five or ten minutes.) Do this as many times as necessary until your puppy relieves himself. Do not assume your puppy has done his business. Seeing is believing, and you need to see your puppy empty his bladder or bowels. You will need to repeat this routine many, many times throughout the day and again just before you go to bed at night.

Because playtime is so special for Bostons, allow it only after your dogs have relieved themselves in the appropriate spot when you go out with them.

Investing in the Future

Why go to all this trouble? The importance of going with your puppy and watching him has many important purposes. First, if your puppy is on leash, you can take him to the same spot each time he needs to eliminate. This helps establish the habit of using a certain area of your yard. This also helps to keep your puppy on track and prevent him from getting too distracted with the variety of sights, smells, and sounds. Puppies are naturally curious and easily distracted. While sniffing the ground usually helps to speed up the process, if your puppy gets too distracted and forgets to go when you bring him back indoors and he is no longer distracted, he will feel a sudden urge to go -- and it is highly likely that he will go on your carpet.

In addition, by going outside with your puppy, you can praise him for doing what you want, which is going to the bathroom outdoors. Praise will help your puppy to understand exactly what you want and will maximize the learning process.

Almost, but Not Quite

Owners often err by thinking their puppy is housetrained when it is really only wishful thinking on their part. Puppies between the ages of eight and ten weeks do not show signs of having to urinate. When they have to go, they go right away—often stopping to urinate in the middle of a play session. It is unrealistic to expect your puppy to stop what he is doing and tell you that he needs to go outside. More often than not, your puppy won't realize he has to go until he is already going. Your job for the next six months, or longer depending on the puppy, is to keep an eye on your puppy and anticipate his bathroom needs.

Around 10 or 12 weeks of age, a puppy will start to exhibit signs—warning signals that he is about to urinate or defecate—by circling, making crying noises, sniffing the floor, or arching his back. Oftentimes, his tail will come up or he might stand by the door. This is where owners get overconfident and think they are home free. These are signs that your puppy is learning, not that he is housetrained. Now more than ever you need to remain diligent and stick to the program. And, you can begin teaching him which signal to use to let you know he needs to go outside by reinforcing any or all of the signals.

By following these simple steps, your puppy will learn through repetition and consistency to relieve himself outdoors. Patience and consistency are the keys to housetraining. There are no shortcuts. Don't backslide or slack off. You will only be creating problems that will exist for many years to come. The more your puppy can urinate and defecate outdoors, the quicker he will learn and the happier you will be.

Accidents Will Happen

While it is in yours and your dog's best interest to keep indoor accidents to a minimum, few owners escape puppy rearing without an accident here or there. If an accident does happen, consider it your fault and be more observant in the future. Never scold or hit your puppy and never, ever rub his nose in the mess. Those are not housetraining techniques, they are crimes in progress. Punishing, yelling, or otherwise berating your puppy will only confuse him and prolong the housetraining process.

Dogs live in the moment. Young or old, they do not have the mental wherewithal to associate the punishment they are receiving with an earlier act of urinating on the floor. When you scold your puppy, your puppy will display a submissive response. He is reacting to your mannerisms and tone of voice. Most owners tend to believe their puppy's submissive demeanor is because he understands he did something wrong.

Paper Training as an Alternative

While crate training is one of the quickest and most efficient methods of housetraining, in some situations it might not be entirely possible. If, for instance, you live in a high-rise apartment building, running down 20 flights of stairs every hour to potty your puppy presents its own unique challenges. An option you might want to consider is paper training, rather than crate training, as an alternative method of housetraining.

The concept behind paper training is similar to taking your puppy to the same spot outdoors each time. Rather

No Yelling at Accidents

The sooner you recognize that a puppy does not have the capacity to make the connection in his mind between your angry demeanor and his urinating on the floor three minutes or two hours ago, the sooner you can move forward and expedite the housetraining process. Furthermore, scolding, punishing, or berating your puppy is counterproductive to building a solid, trusting, and mutually respectful relationship.

than going outside, you teach your puppy to eliminate on sheets of newspaper. In the beginning, the newspaper covers most of the floor, preferably a surface such as linoleum or tile that is easily cleaned and disinfected. As your puppy learns to relieve himself on the paper, you gradually begin decreasing the amount of floor space covered by paper until the puppy is eliminating on a piece of paper about the size of one sheet of newspaper. As your puppy matures and begins to hold his bladder for longer and longer periods of time, you begin teaching him to eliminate outdoors. The biggest drawback with this technique is that for several months your puppy is allowed to relieve himself indoors. Once he begins to mature and can hold his bladder for longer periods, you still need to go through the process of teaching him to relieve himself outdoors. If your puppy falls into the habit of eliminating indoors it can be a very difficult habit to break.

If you have a balcony that is puppy-proofed and 100-percent puppy safe, you can try placing a piece of indoor/outdoor carpet, newspaper, or cat box–type setup on the balcony and teach your puppy to eliminate outdoors rather than on the newspaper indoors. As with the crate-training technique, you will need to go with your puppy and show him where to eliminate, and then praise and reward him for doing so.

A playpen, exercise pen, or strategically placed baby gates, can work wonders for limiting your puppy's access to certain areas of the house while he is being housetrained. If an accident does happen, at least it is confined to a small area.

Housetraining Tips

- Maintain a regular feeding schedule with meal times spaced evenly throughout the day. What goes in on a regular basis will come out on a regular basis.
- As a general rule, puppies need to relieve themselves

about 15 to 20 minutes after drinking water and 30 minutes after eating.

- Keep a mental note (or write it down if necessary) of when your puppy eats and drinks, and what your puppy is doing each time he goes to the bathroom. If you know what is normal behavior for your puppy, you'll know when something is out of the ordinary.

- To help you and your puppy sleep through the night, limit your puppy's food and water intake approximately one hour before you turn out the lights. This will help to insure his bladder and bowels are empty. Note: do not restrict water intake during the day, but do avoid allowing your puppy to drink heavily as bedtime approaches.

- Choose a quality food designed for your puppy's needs and try to stick with it, provided there are no

Puppies raised on paper may quickly take to housetraining on shredded newspaper, which may be more convenient for you.

problems. Avoid changing brands from week to week, especially during the housetraining phase. Changing foods can upset your puppy's digestive tract and complicate the housetraining process. If you must change foods, do it gradually.

- Cheaper foods are not always the best buy. Premium foods cost more but may be more cost-effective since you don't need to serve as much to fulfill your puppy's nutritional needs. It's also more digestible, often resulting in smaller stool.
- Feed the same amount of food at each feeding. Pick up any uneaten food after 15 minutes. This keeps your puppy's digestive tract on a regular schedule and helps to prevent finicky eating habits.
- Avoid free-feeding—putting your puppy's food bowl on the floor and allowing him to nibble throughout the day, at his leisure.
- Despite what your close friends and in-laws say, most puppies are not thoroughly and reliably housetrained until they are seven or eight months of age—some even a year old.

SOCIALIZATION

There are certain periods in a puppy's life that are critical in his social development. What happens within these individual stages has an enormous impact on his future behavior as an adult. A responsible breeder will take advantage of these critical periods to maximize a puppy's future, foster his individual personality, and instill desired behaviors.

The Breeder's Role

The socialization period, when your puppy is between 5 and 16 weeks of age, is pivotal in your puppy's development. During the first few weeks of this stage, the main emphasis of socialization begins to shift from your puppy's canine mother and his littermates toward human beings and the world beyond the whelping box. It is the primary time when your Boston learns to adjust and interact to the presence of people in his life.

By the time your Boston puppy is ready to begin his new life at your home, usually between seven and eight weeks of age, the process of socialization will have already begun. The breeder will have seen your puppy through the neonatal and transitional periods and halfway through the critical socialization period. During this time, responsible and knowledgeable breeders will ensure their litters are handled daily in order to accustom them to human contact and to imprint trust. They will make sure the puppies receive individual attention and are exposed to a variety of sights and smells in a safe and stress-free environment. Many breeders will have accustomed their young puppies to crates, thereby facilitating the crate-training process.

This is why you need to make careful choices about where you acquire your Boston Terrier. How your puppy is managed during the socialization period has a tremendous impact on how he reacts and interacts to various situations and people as an adult dog,

Your Role

Your job begins the day your puppy arrives at your home. There is much to accomplish and a very small window of opportunity, so it is important to maximize your time and use it wisely. There are important socialization skills your Boston must learn between 8 and 16 weeks of age. Once this small window of opportunity has closed, it can never be reopened. The lessons learned during this stage will help your Boston develop the socialization skills and coping mechanisms necessary to grow into a mentally sound and confident adult dog. If you dawdle or squander your opportunities during this critical time, your puppy will suffer in the long run. You run the risk of having your Boston develop bad habits and associations that are difficult, if not impossible, to correct later in life.

As the owner of a new Boston puppy, you are assuming the role of parent and pack leader. You are assuming an enormous responsibility that includes protecting him from bad or traumatic experiences while simultaneously instilling desired behaviors, fostering his unique personality, and providing him with every opportunity to grow into a well-adjusted, mentally confident adult dog.

Before taking your puppy outdoors and around other animals, you should consult your veterinarian about any necessary puppy vaccinations to ensure that your Boston Terrier is protected from diseases. Then, in a fun, safe, and stress-free environment, you will want to begin exposing your Boston to a wide variety of people, including babies in strollers, kids on bicycles, women carrying bags, men in floppy hats, and so forth.

You should expose your puppy to the clapping of hands, the jingling of keys, and the clatter of dog bowls. He should explore a variety of surfaces, including grass, cement, gravel, tile, carpet, linoleum, sand, and dirt. He should be exposed to stairways, wheelchair ramps, paper bags blowing in the wind, wind chimes, and horns honking. Let your puppy play in and around empty boxes, tunnels, or buckets. Allow him to investigate trees, rocks, bushes, branches, leaves, and fallen fruit. He should explore bugs, and other animal odors, pastures, wooded areas, city sidewalks, and sandy beaches.

Enlarge your puppy's world and challenge his curiosity by taking him for rides in the car and walks in the park. Allow him to explore the many sights, sounds, and smells of a local dog show. Take him to the veterinarian's office or the local groomer for a cookie and a kiss. If you are interested in canine competition, expose him in a controlled atmosphere

Accidents are bound to happen during the housetraining process. Some breeds are more challenging than others. Small breeds, submissive or stressed puppies, and heavily kenneled puppies, can be especially challenging. You should seek veterinary assistance if you observe any of the following conditions: change in color or odor of urine; change in frequency of urination; sudden change in the number of accidents; or a sweet or foul odor to the puppy.

Bostons who have been well socialized can be taken almost anywhere and are reliable around strangers and in strange environments.

to the scents and sounds that he will encounter later in competition, such as agility or obedience equipment.

As your puppy's guardian of safety and well-being, you will want to protect your puppy from potentially harmful or fearful situations, yet not coddle or reward fearful behavior. You will want to observe your puppy's reactions to different situations. Watch his ears and tail and body posture. Is he fearful? Apprehensive? Courageous? Dominant? Submissive? By understanding and reading your Boston's body language, you will be better able to evaluate and adjust the situation accordingly. For instance, if your Boston was raised in a childless environment, a room full of noisy, rambunctious children may be overwhelming or downright scary. By coddling or otherwise rewarding a puppy that shows fear, you are reinforcing his fear. Try modifying or restricting the exposure to one quiet, well-behaved child in the beginning until your puppy's confidence can handle more. When your puppy is brave, praise and reinforce him for being brave and inquisitive.

DISCIPLINING YOUR BOSTON

No discussion on training or problem behaviors would be complete without a word or two about disciplining your

Boston. Only rarely should you need to discipline or correct a young puppy. The majority of your interactions should be positive and fun as you work toward building a solid human/canine relationship by instilling desired behaviors, discouraging undesired behaviors, and fostering his particular personality. Managing your Boston so he does not develop bad behaviors is critical.

It is much easier to create good habits through smart management and positive motivation than it is to go back and fix bad habits. You should take every opportunity to manipulate situations so your dog does the right thing and can be rewarded. This is the essence of positive motivation and reinforcement. If left to their own devices, Boston Terriers, like most puppies and adult dogs, will do what is in their best interest and that is seldom, if ever, conducive to living in a domesticated environment.

Before dogs were domesticated they lived in packs where their survival was dependent on a hierarchal system. To coexist peacefully and guarantee their survival, the pack needed a clear chain of command. In the domesticated society your home represents, you must always be the top dog. Your Boston's position in the chain of command should always lie below you. This is a hard concept for some owners to grasp, but it is pivotal if you want your Boston Terrier to grow into a well-behaved dog rather than an unruly hooligan.

What Is a Correction?

During the adolescent stage, when your puppy begins to assert himself—perhaps challenging the chain of command—you may need to discipline him from time to time. Doing so correctly and effectively will ensure that your Boston puppy grows into a well-behaved adult dog that is a joy to live with, both at home and in public. Discipline should never be the staple of your puppy's training or the first line of defense when things begin to go wrong. Corrections should be reserved for completely unacceptable behaviors, such as when your Boston is biting you, your kids, or another dog. This type of behavior, if left unchecked, can be disastrous. Biting is unacceptable and should be stopped immediately, otherwise it is highly likely your Boston will repeat the behavior as he grows and matures.

Also in adolescence, your Boston may decide to deliberately ignore your command because he would rather sniff a bug, play with his canine buddies, chew on a bone, or any one of the myriad canine activities. An immediate correction will teach your Boston that he must respond to you when given a command. That said, before correcting your Boston you must be absolutely certain your dog thoroughly understands and has heard the command.

It does not matter if your Boston is six months or three years old, if you have not taught him the command, such as coming when called, it is unfair to correct him for not complying. You cannot correct your Boston for something he has not learned. To do so is unfair and undermines the foundation on which a trusting human/canine relationship is built. When you correct a dog that does not understand a command or that is confused or worried, he will learn to fear rather than trust you.

Correcting or disciplining your Boston does not mean he is bad. You are correcting the wrong choice and making the right choice happen. What constitutes discipline is different for every Boston. The amount of discipline used will depend on your Boston's temperament. For

Praise your puppy for being brave and inquisitive. It will boost his self-confidence.

some Bostons, a change in your tone of voice coupled with an *Aaagh!* is enough. For bolder Bostons, a stern *No!* may be in order.

A correction given with the appropriate amount of force and proper timing will eliminate the wrong behavior. A good guideline is to always use enough discipline so your dog gets the message the first time. Then move on. Of course, that is often easier said than done. You will need to watch the effect the correction has on your Boston. If you overcorrect, it is highly likely you will scare or possibly injure your Boston, and he may be a bit leery of you. If the correction is too light, your Boston is likely to continue with the behavior for which he was being corrected. If you repeat the correction multiple times without a response, you are nagging. When you nag your Boston with corrections, he will quickly learn to ignore you. If your Boston stops the offensive behavior after one or two corrections, you have the correction level about right.

When it comes to disciplining her brood, a mother does it best. A bitch is quite adept at making a correction with the precise amount of harshness necessary to make her point. The correction is immediate, startling, and effective. Ninety-nine percent of the time, her puppies get the message the first time, and the offensive behavior stops immediately. A bitch rarely, if ever, under-corrects or overcorrects her babies. Once the correction is completed, she never holds a grudge or denies her puppies love and affection, food, or maternal care, and neither should you. Once you issue a cor-

rection, it is important that your Boston understand it is the unwanted behavior to which you object. Once you correct your dog, play with him for a few seconds to take his mind off the correction, and restore his happy attitude. Once you have your dog's full attention, give the command again, and when he responds, reward him with plenty of praise.

You may find that when your Boston reaches adolescence he doesn't listen as well as he should. Correct him appropriately.

PROBLEM BEHAVIORS

In a perfect world, puppies and adult dogs would never get into trouble. In the real world, however, it is unrealistic to expect any dog to go through its entire life without getting into some sort of mischief or developing an annoying habit or two. It is important to remember that dogs, like kids, are first and foremost individuals. No two are alike, and they must be treated as individuals in order to maximize their potential. Their temperaments can fall within a broad range of characteristics, and they can develop their own quirks and idiosyncrasies.

It is much easier to create and foster good habits than it is to cure bad ones. Once you have a keen sense of your Boston's personality, and you are aware of the predispositions he is likely to have inherited, you can develop a training program that encourages desired behaviors and discourages unwanted ones.

Excessive Barking

Overall, the Boston Terrier is by no means a noisy dog. However, it is natural for dogs to bark or otherwise vocalize. They bark for a variety of reasons. They bark when they get excited, when they are playing with other dogs, when the doorbell rings, and to greet you when you arrive home. If you have done enough proper socialization, your Boston will not regard every little noise or visitor as a threat.

Your Boston's barking will hopefully be reasonable and appropriate, such as to alert you to suspicious intruders or unexpected visitors. Most well-socialized adult dogs have an innate desire to protect their territory and will alert bark without being taught to do so. Also, if your Boston can be quieted with a single command, you probably do not have much to worry about with respect to incessant barking. Problems arise when your dog is too hyped up to stop barking. Therefore, it is best to curtail any problems immediately. This includes never encouraging your Boston to bark. For instance, when the doorbell rings, avoid asking your Boston, "Who's there?" or "Let's go see!" This can excite your Boston and encourage him to bark. It may seem like a fun game when he is ten or twelve weeks old, but it is a difficult and annoying behavior to stop once it becomes ingrained.

If your puppy is barking as an attention-seeking behavior, it is best to ignore him until he quiets. Then calmly praise him. Whatever you do, do not verbally or physically acknowledge your dog's barking. By shouting "No" or "Be quiet," the dog is likely to think you are joining in. This will only encourage the unwanted behavior.

Equally important, in a dog's mind negative attention is better than no attention at all. By verbally responding to your dog, you are inadvertently giving the dog what he wants, which is attention. As long as everyone in the family ignores the attention-seeking barking, your dog is likely to lose interest and quickly give it up as a fruitless venture that does not offer any reward.

It is best not to soothe or otherwise coddle your Boston when he is barking. This, too, will inadvertently encourage the unwanted behavior. If your dog is barking and you are telling him, "It's okay, honey. Mommy loves you," the dog may think he is being rewarded for barking. In the dog's mind, he is thinking, "When I bark, my mom tells me it's okay. So I should keep barking." You are inadvertently encouraging the behavior.

Most barking problems can be avoided if you plan ahead and have a clear picture of the behaviors you will and will not accept. However, if your Boston has already developed a barking problem and is well on his way to wearing out his welcome, you can try a shaker can as a training aid coupled with positive reinforcement.

Using a Shaker Can

The concept behind a shaker can is that it makes a lot of noise and interrupts the dog's barking. Once the dog's barking behavior is interrupted, you can praise and reward him for not barking. Shaker cans are easily constructed using an empty soda can. Simply fill it with a dozen or so coins or small pebbles and tape the opening closed. As soon as your Boston begins to bark—for instance, when the doorbell rings—immediately give a command, such as Quiet, Enough, or No Bark, and shake the can. The noise will startle the dog and interrupt his barking. When he stops barking, immediately praise him. You can also reinforce the behavior with a tidbit of food, but be sure to do so when the dog is *not* barking. Otherwise, you will be teaching the wrong association and inadvertently reinforcing the barking.

Be sure to keep multiple shaker cans strategically placed around the house—near the telephone, front door, bedroom, living room, etc.—for convenience and accessibility. A word of caution: Be sure to place the shaker cans out of your dog's reach. Aluminum cans are sharp and dangerous when punctured or torn. Boston Terriers, curious creatures that they are, can cause serious damage to their teeth, tongues, mouths, and stomachs if they chew on the can. Once a Boston gets the can open, he may try to swallow the coins, which presents a potential choking hazard. Most important, never throw the can—or any other objects—at your Boston Terrier. You may injure or frighten him, and he will most likely learn to fear you.

Digging

Dogs love to dig. They find it both necessary and pleasurable. Unfortunately, their idea of fun can cause you a significant amount of frustration and heartache, especially when your precious pooch digs under your newly planted rose bushes. If you're the type of owner who doesn't care if your four-legged friend's full-time job is excavating your yard, you've nothing to worry about. Let him dig away, provided, of course, it's safe for him to do so. However, if you prefer not to have potholes in your garden and lawn, prevention is the best solution.

Most often, dogs will dig out of frustration or boredom. Some dig holes to bury their favorite toys or bones. Others will dig in order to find a cool spot to escape the heat.

Do something that will stimulate his mind, burn excess energy, and tire him out. Use your imagination to come up with fun games. For instance, purchase a food-dispensing puzzle that allows him to exercise his brain as he tries to outsmart the toy. There are chew toys that can be stuffed with squeeze cheese or peanut butter, and will provide your Boston with hours of entertainment. Or, play fun *Find It* games where you hide a tasty tidbit of food under a small box or dish and encourage him to find it. Play hide-and-seek games where you encourage him to find you.

Dogs also like to dig in fresh soil and newly fertilized gardens, and they are frequently attracted to the smell of chicken and steer manure. The best solution for digging in gardens and flower boxes is prevention. Do not allow your Boston free access to the garden areas where he can dig and wreak havoc. An alternative is to install a small fence around the garden, or put chicken wire under the soil so digging becomes less productive and rewarding for the dog.

Not Coming When Called

Boston Terriers that run away from their owners or refuse to come when called can create an enormous amount of

If you think your Boston is digging out of boredom, rather than scold him, take him for a walk, play ball with him, take him to an obedience class, or enroll him in an agility class. Participate in an activity that is interactive.

If your Boston Terrier is digging to find a cool spot to escape the heat, his digging is the least of your problems. Bostons cannot tolerate hot weather. You need to get him out of the heat and provide him with a cool spot, such as an air-conditioned room or a cool grassy area with plenty of shade.

If you want your dogs to come to you when you call, reward them for it while training. They need to associate coming to you with all good things.

frustration and angst for their owners. The good news is that it is one of the easiest problems to solve. The key is to never allow your puppy to be put in a situation where he is allowed to develop the bad habit of running off. Each and every time you go outside, your puppy should be dragging his leash or a lightweight long-line. If your puppy starts to wander off, simply step on the long-line and reel him back in.

If your adult dog has already developed the annoying habit of running off or ignoring your Come command, a leash or long-line will prevent him from continuing to do so. You will then need to go back and reteach him to Come when called. You should also never get in the habit of chasing your puppy, or allowing your kids to chase your puppy. This teaches the dog to run away from you.

Chewing

It is hard to imagine an adorable Boston puppy that weighs only a few pounds as a one-dog demolition team. However, don't let their cute looks and small stature deceive you. Boston puppies, like most puppies, can be incredibly aggressive chewers and wreak havoc in your household. They can destroy drywall, carpet, drapes, and linoleum. They can turn your favorite pillows into confetti, shred your bedspread, destroy electrical cords and potted plants. They will gladly shred magazines and books and anything else they can get their teeth on—and that's just in the 15 minutes it takes you to drive to the post office and back!

If you must leave—even for two minutes—take your Boston with you or confine him in a crate, exercise pen, or kennel. Do not put your Boston in a position where he can develop bad habits. This point cannot be emphasized enough. Puppies chew, especially when they are teething. If you leave your Boston unattended while you run to the mailbox or take a quick shower, you shouldn't be surprised when you find the heel missing off your favorite pair of leather shoes.

Teething

Around four weeks of age, puppies begin to develop their baby teeth—also known as deciduous teeth or milk teeth. Teething is the process of growing baby teeth. The process ends when a dog's permanent teeth are in place. Teething varies from puppy to puppy with most puppies undergoing some form of continuous teething until they are about nine months of age. Baby teeth are either erupting or being replaced by permanent teeth.

A puppy's baby teeth erupt from the gum line and are small and very sharp. The first teeth to come in are the canine teeth and incisors, followed by the premolars and molars.

Around 14 or 16 weeks of age, puppies begin shedding their baby teeth as the permanent teeth begin pushing up under the baby teeth. This stimulates an uncontrollable urge to chew as a means of relieving some of the discomfort, and as a way to facilitate the removal of their baby teeth.

Around four to six months of age, the baby teeth are gradually replaced with permanent teeth. This brings on another wave of chewing, sometimes referred to as exploratory chewing. During this stage, puppies are exploring their environment. Much like human babies, they are inquisitive and explore their surroundings by putting anything and everything in their mouths. This stage usually lasts until the dog is about one year old. However, some Boston owners claim their dogs have been as old as three before they are completely through the chewing stage.

It's important to keep in mind that dogs have no sense of value. They do not have the mental wherewithal to distinguish between the leg on your grandmother's antique Chippendale table and an old stick they found in the yard. They do not know the difference between an electrical cord and a designated chew toy. If your Boston does not have an assortment of appropriate chew toys, he will actively try to find something, which can mean furniture legs, shoes, socks, pillows, electrical cords, and even your pants legs, arms, and hands.

PROBLEM PREVENTION

Few owners escape canine ownership without losing a slipper, a pair of rubber galoshes, or a potted plant. Puppies are going to chew. It's a fact of life. However, the key to minimizing destruction and preventing bad habits is management. Never allow your puppy to be put in a position where he can get himself into trouble or develop bad habits. Any puppy left unsupervised is trouble looking for someplace to happen.

If you allow your puppy to have free run of the house, you shouldn't be surprised when you come home to find epic amounts of destruction. It is equally unfair to scold or otherwise punish a puppy for your temporary lapse of good judgment. Therefore, to foster good habits and minimize destructive behaviors, follow these simply guidelines:

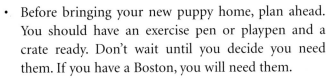

Teach Your Puppy Right From Wrong

If you allow your Boston puppy supervised excursions into the rest of the house, you will be able to monitor his whereabouts and, in the process, provide him with appropriate chew toys. If, for instance, you are watching television, have one or two chew toys available for your puppy. You may need to encourage him by showing him the toy. When you see him settle down to chew on it, calmly praise him. Then allow him to chew without interruption. You can try tethering him to the leg of the couch or coffee table with a lightweight leash to prevent him from wandering off.

Until your puppy is reliable, it is wise not to give him free run of the house. Remember, puppies are individuals. It is impossible to arbitrarily put an age on when a puppy is well trained. Some puppies have a stronger desire to chew than others. A general guideline is about one year of age. However, much of this will also depend on how conscientious and committed you are to managing your puppy's environment, instilling good behaviors, and discouraging unwanted behaviors.

As your puppy grows and matures, his desire to chew will diminish. It is important, however, to continue giving him bones and chew toys throughout his life to exercise his jaws, keep his teeth clean, and entertain him for a few hours.

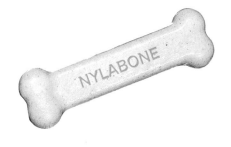

- Before bringing your new puppy home, plan ahead. You should have an exercise pen or playpen and a crate ready. Don't wait until you decide you need them. If you have a Boston, you will need them.

- When you can't keep a constant watch on your puppy, keep him confined in an exercise pen, play pen, crate, or puppy-proofed area with his favorite chew toy. This includes when you need to jump in the shower for five minutes, while you are making dinner, or when you dash outside for two seconds to move the sprinkler.

- Once your puppy arrives at your home, know where he is and what he is doing at all times. You would never dream of taking your eyes off a toddler, and you should not take your eyes off a Boston Terrier puppy when he is not safely confined.

- Puppy-proof your home. Puppies are ingenious when it comes to finding items to chew on. Pick up anything and everything your puppy is likely to put in his mouth including shoes, purses, jackets, schoolbooks, candles, rugs, electrical cords, dolls, and so forth.

- Make sure your Boston receives plenty of exercise each day. Bostons are lively, energetic dogs that require daily physical and mental stimulation. Lacking appropriate and adequate exercise, they will release pent up energy through chewing, digging, or barking.

THE IMPORTANCE OF CHEW TOYS

There are a variety of chew toys available in all sizes and

shapes that will entertain your Boston for an hour or two. Chew toys will satisfy your puppy's need to gnaw on something while diverting him from chewing on inappropriate items. While some chew toys are better than others, there is no scientific formula for finding the right chew toy. Most times it's a matter of trial and error. Avoid toys or bones that are too hard and may crack your dog's teeth, or ones that are too small or break apart and present choking hazards.

Rigid Nylon and Hard Rubber

Specially designed rigid nylon and rubber bones and toys are excellent for satisfying your puppy's need to chew. Hard and durable, they are perfect for even the most tenacious and aggressive chewer. Some chew toys are hollow so you can stuff them with tasty treats, such as peanut butter or squeeze cheese, making them even more fun for your Boston. Some are flavored with meat or vegetable juices. Be sure to purchase bones and toys that are designed to withstand virtually any impact without cracking or breaking, such as those made by Nylabone. This helps to prevent your Boston from biting or chewing off chunks, which might be a potential choking hazard.

Rope Toys and Tugs

Rope toys and tugs are often made of 100-percent cotton. They are frequently flavored to make them more attractive to your puppy or adult dog. Some have plaque-fighting fluoride floss woven into the rope to deep-clean your dog's teeth and gums. Be careful your puppy cannot shred the cotton ropes, which may be a potential choking hazard.

Cotton tugs and toys can absorb saliva and become laden with bacteria, so be sure to wash your Boston's cotton toys regularly.

Edible Chews

Chew toys are popular with many Boston owners. Chews are available in a wide variety of shapes, sizes, and products, including beef muscle, pig ears, smoked hog hide, dehydrated pig snouts, and tightly rolled rawhide. Some colored rawhide chews can stain carpets and furnishings. Cow hooves, while a popular canine favorite, are hard and can chip or break your dog's teeth.

Plush and Squeaky Toys

Usually made of durable polyester, fleece, or plush fabrics, these toys vary in their durability. Some are easily shredded by the tenacious, seek-and-destroy Bostons that can chew out the squeaky part in record time, while some dogs like to carry them around or snuggle with them. When choosing these toys, opt for the durable models if your puppy is likely to shred, disembowel, and then attempt to consume the innards.

Fresh Foods

A large carrot is often a good chew toy for young puppies. Carrots are tasty, durable, easily digestible, and puppies seem to love them. Stay away from raisins and grapes, which can be toxic in certain quantities.

ADVANCED
TRAINING AND
ACTIVITIES
WITH YOUR BOSTON TERRIER

Boston Terriers are intelligent, energetic, and always up for a bit of fun. That means finding the perfect sport or pastime for you and your Boston is a cinch. After all, there are countless canine activities from which to choose. The physical, mental, and financial demands of canine activities vary dramatically, and how much you are willing to invest is always a personal choice. It may take a few tries at different activities, but chances are there is a canine sport that your Boston will prefer. National clubs and registries, such as the American Kennel Club, Canadian Kennel Club, United Kennel Club, Boston Terrier Club of America, and The Kennel Club, offer a wide variety of all breed and breed-specific canine sports and competitions in which your Boston Terrier can compete.

Training and competing with your Boston Terrier allows you to enhance the human/canine relationship, build a strong and mutually respectful relationship, and have a great deal of fun in the process. You might even ignite the competitive spark and find yourself hooked on canine competitions. If your Boston is not breed quality, don't worry; there are plenty of canine sports you can enter that will showcase your dog's agility, athleticism, and intelligence. Through American Kennel Club-sanctioned events alone you and your Boston can participate in the Canine Good Citizen, Obedience, Rally Obedience, Agility, Tracking, and Conformation.

CANINE GOOD CITIZEN

If you enjoy training your Boston but organized competitions aren't your cup of tea, the American Kennel Club's Canine Good Citizen® (CGC) Program might be a viable alternative. Implemented in 1989, the CGC Program is a public education and certification program designed to encourage owners to develop a positive and worthwhile relationship with their dogs by rewarding responsible dog ownership and good pet manners. While the program does not involve the formality or precision of competitive obedience, it does lay the foundation for good pet manners and is often used as a stepping-stone for other canine activities, such as obedience and agility.

The CGC program is designed to encourage owners to get involved with and train their dogs to have good manners. It is a noncompetitive, 10-part test that evaluates your Boston's

Training for and competing in various activities with your Boston will deepen your relationship.

behavior in practical situations at home, in public, and in the presence of unfamiliar people and other dogs. The pass or fail test is designed to test a Boston's reaction to distractions, friendly strangers, and supervised isolation. Additionally, a Boston Terrier must sit politely while being petted, walk on a loose leash, walk through a crowd, and respond to basic obedience commands including sit, down, stay, and come. The evaluator also inspects the dog to determine if he is clean and groomed. Both purebred and mixed-breed dogs are eligible to participate. While there is no age limit, dogs must be old enough to have received their immunizations.

FORMAL OBEDIENCE

Every aspect of dog ownership involves some form of obedience training, yet the obedience ring seldom receives the publicity and media attention of other canine events. An obedience trial goes well beyond the CGC program and tests your Boston's ability to perform a prescribed set of exercises in a formal environment. The obedience ring is a showcase for dogs and owners who have trained diligently to work in unison, obey specific commands, and follow speci-fied exercises in a competitive venue. One might compare it to the formal and elegant equine dressage tests with owners achieving a harmonious relationship with their dogs, all the while observing meticulous attention to minute details.

In addition to enriching the bond and relationship between a dog and handler, obedience training is designed to emphasize "the usefulness of purebred dogs as the ulti-mate companion and helpmate to man, and as a means of recognizing that dogs have been trained to behave in the home, in public places, and in the presence of other dogs."

The Novice Level

Novice obedience is the first level of competitive obedience and tests a dog's ability to follow basic obedience commands.

The dog is required to heel on and off leash at a normal, fast, and slow pace; come when called; stand for a physical examination by the judge; and do a sit-stay and a down-stay with other dogs. Other than giving commands, handlers are not allowed to talk to their dog during the exercises, nor are they allowed to use toys, treats, or other training aids inside the ring.

A dog must earn a score of 170 or better out of a possi-ble 200, and must earn at least 50 percent of the allowable points in each exercise. Each time a dog receives a qualifying score he receives a *leg* toward his title. When he receives three legs under three different judges, he receives a Companion Dog (CD) title.

The Open Level

The Open class is the second level of competition and only dogs that have earned a CD title are eligible to compete. The Open class is quite a bit more difficult than the Novice class because all exercises are performed off leash. A dog will be required to do similar heelwork exercises as in the Novice class, as well as a retrieve exercise, a drop on recall, a high jump, broad jump, and a sit-stay and down-stay with other dogs while the handlers are out of sight. Again, a Boston Terrier will need to receive a qualifying score of 170 out of a possible 200 under three different judges, and must earn at least 50 percent of the allowable points in each category to receive a Companion Dog Excellent (CDX) title.

To compete at the Utility level of obedience, your Boston will need to pass a scent discrimination test where he has to choose the correct article from a group of similar items.

Obedience titles are difficult—but not impossible—to attain. In 2004, Boston Terriers earned 21 CDs, 5 CDXs, and 2 UDs at AKC competitions.

The Utility Level

Utility is the final and most difficult and challenging level of training. A dog must have earned a CD and CDX title in order to compete in the Utility class. The exercises include scent discrimination, directed jumping, retrieving, hand signals, and a moving stand and examination. As with the other classes, a dog will need to receive three qualifying scores under three different judges to receive a Utility Dog (UD) title.

If you've gotten this far, you are seriously committed to the sport of obedience, and you may decide to work toward a Utility Dog Excellent or Obedience Trial Championship title. A UD dog that continues to compete and earn qualifying scores in both Open B and Utility B classes at ten shows receives the Utility Dog Excellent title.

The Ultimate OTCH

An Obedience Trial Champion (OTCH) title is regarded by serious enthusiasts as the Holy Grail; the *creme de la creme* of obedience competition. While it is considered the most prestigious title, it has also proven to be the most elusive crown since its inception in 1977.

To receive an OTCH, a dog must earn 100 championship

Get a Checkup First

Before beginning any physically challenging activity with your Boston, it is prudent to take him to a veterinarian for a thorough checkup and examination. The breed's facial structure can cause some dogs to have difficulty breathing in warm temperatures and during physical activities. Joint problems, such as luxating patellas (slipped knees), are common in some Bostons and should be of paramount importance and concern for owners. They may preclude your Boston from some of the more physically demanding activities. Low-stress activities are wonderful for puppies, but young dogs (generally under the age of two) should not be allowed to jump. Too much pressure on developing joints and limbs can injure your puppy and lead to lifelong problems.

points, including earning a first place in Utility B with at least three dogs in the class, a first place in Open B with at least six dogs in competition, and a first place in either of the previous situations. The three first-place finishes must also be under three different judges. Points are earned similarly to the breed ring in that they are based on a schedule of points established by the AKC.

The best way to get involved in obedience is to sign up for dog obedience class or join a local dog obedience club. If you are interested in the sport of competitive obedience, it is helpful to find a trainer who competes in the sport and teaches competitive obedience classes.

RALLY OBEDIENCE

Rally obedience is the newest AKC event. While it has been around for about three years as a non-regular class, it finally became a regular class on January 1, 2005. It is a combination of agility and obedience. However, the emphasis is less on speed and precision and more on how well a dog and handler perform together as a team. It was created with the average dog owner in mind and as a means to help promote a positive human/canine relationship, with an emphasis on fun and excitement. It also takes the pressure off of competing, while still allowing owners to showcase their Bostons' obedience skills.

In rally obedience, the dog and handler move through a course that has been designed by the rally judge. The dog and handler proceed at their own pace through a course of designated stations—between 10 and 20 stations, depending on the level. Each of these stations has a sign providing instructions regarding the skill that is to be performed, such as Halt and Sit; Halt, Sit, and Down; Right Turn; About Right Turn; or while heeling, perform a 270-degree left turn.

Unlike traditional obedience competitions, handlers are permitted to talk to their dogs, use praise, clap their hands, pat their legs, or use any verbal means of communication and body language throughout the performance. Handlers may not touch their dog or make physical corrections. Any dog that is eligible for AKC registration can enter Rally obedience.

AGILITY

Agility is one of the fastest growing sports for dogs, and one of the most exciting, fast-paced canine sports for spectators. It is an extension of obedience, yet without all the formality and precision. Agility courses are more reminiscent of equestrian Grand Prix courses that include assorted jumps and hurdles. In agility, dogs demonstrate their agile nature and versatility by maneuvering through a timed obstacle course of jumps, tunnels, A-frames, weave poles, teeter-totters, ramps, and a pause box. Unlike obedience, agility handlers are permitted to talk to their dogs, and even give multiple commands.

A good agility handler is like a navigator who aims the dog toward each successive obstacle while trying to regulate the dog's speed and precision—and, of course, trying to stay out of the way of a fast-performing dog. A perfect score in any class is 100, and competitors are faulted if they go over the allotted course time or receive a penalty, such as taking an obstacle out of sequence, missing a contact zone, touching the dog, and so forth.

All-breed agility trials are the most common type of trial and are open to all AKC breeds and varieties of dogs. Specialty trials are restricted to dogs of a specific breed or varieties of one breed. There are two types of classes offered at an agility trial: Standard and Jumpers with Weaves. The Standard class has a pause box and contact obstacles—those yellow contact zones at each end of the obstacle. The dog must place at least one paw in the contact zone—otherwise, he receives a fault. The goal is to encourage safety in training and in running the course. The Jumpers with Weaves class also has a variety of obstacles but does not have contact obstacles or a pause box that slow the competitor's forward momentum. Within each agility class there are different levels of competition:

• Novice: for the dog that is just starting in agility. There are 13 to 15 obstacles on the course, and the focus is on

Boston Terrier owners are eager agility competitors. In 2004, over 100 earned titles in AKC-sanctioned events ranging from Novice to MACH 2!

The History of Agility
The origin of Agility can be traced across the Atlantic to Great Britain. The sport originated in 1978 as a small-scale demonstration in the main ring at the prestigious Crufts Dog Show. The show committee wanted an entertaining event to fill the spare time between the Obedience championships and the Group judging. As a result, John Varley and Peter Meanwell designed a challenging obstacle course, borrowing many elements from equestrian events. The challenging obstacles and fast-paced dogs hooked spectators—and the rest, as they say, is history.

completing each obstacle with a minimum of handling skill required.

- Open: for the dog that has completed the Novice level. There are 16 to 18 obstacles on the course, and the degree of difficultly increases. The Open class also requires significantly more handling skills than the Novice class.
- Excellent: for the dog that has completed the Open level. There are 18 to 20 obstacles, the degree of difficult increases significantly, and the focus is to provide competitors with the opportunity to demonstrate their superior training, communication, and handling skills.

For the die-hard agility competitor, the Master Agility Champion Title (MACH) is the pinnacle of agility competition. To achieve a MACH title, a dog must exhibit speed and consistency on the agility course. They must receive a minimum of 750 champion points and 20 double-qualifying scores from the Excellent B Standard or Excellent B Jumpers and Weaves class. To put it in layman terms: handlers receive one champion point for each full second under the standard course time. They can double the championship points received if they place first in their class. It's challenging, but not impossible.

The best way to get started in agility is to join a local dog-training club or visit an agility training facility.

TRACKING

The first AKC-licensed tracking test took place on June 13, 1936. Today, tracking is a popular sport that tests a Boston Terrier's ability to recognize and track a human scent over varying terrains and climatic changes. It is designed to showcase a dog's intelligence and extremely high level of scent capability. The goal is for the dog to follow a scented track and locate an article left at the end of the trail by a track layer.

Boston Terriers can earn three different tracking titles:

Fast-paced, exciting agility can tire out even the most enthusiastic Boston. This one is done for the day!

Tracking Dog (TD), Tracking Dog Excellent (TDX), and Variable Surface Tracking (VST). If a Boston successfully completes all three tracking titles, he earns the prestigious title of Champion Tracker (CT).

For a Boston to earn a TD title, the dog must follow a track laid by a human track layer. The track must be 440 to 500 yards with three to five changes of direction, and the track must be *aged* at least 30 minutes but not more than two hours before the dog can begin scenting (following the track).

A TDX title is the next level and is slightly more difficult than a TD. It is earned when a Boston follows a track that is between 800 and 1,000 yards and between three and five hours old. The TDX track must have five to seven directional changes and also includes the additional challenge of human cross tracks, which, as the name implies, is a human track that crosses the primary track. A dog must also locate four articles rather than the one article required for a TD.

TD and TDX tracks are laid through open fields and wilderness areas and include varying terrain conditions, such as gullies, plowed land, woods, and vegetation. However, urban sprawl has severely limited those spaces in some parts of the country. As a result, the Variable Surface

Tracking (VST) title was designed to utilize industrial and office parks, college campuses, and so forth. To earn a VST title, dogs must first have a TD title, and they must follow a track that is 600 to 800 yards in length and between three to five hours old. The track may take them down a street, between buildings, across a college campus, asphalt parking lot, concrete sidewalk, and the like.

Unlike obedience and agility titles that require a dog and handler to qualify three times, a Boston Terrier only needs to complete one track successfully to earn each title. If you and your Boston love the great outdoors—tracking might be the sport for you. The best way to get involved in tracking is to contact a local dog obedience club or a national organization, such as the Boston Terrier Club of America, American Kennel Club, or Canadian Kennel Club.

CONFORMATION EVENTS (DOG SHOWS)

Conformation shows (dog shows) are the signature events of the competitive dog world. The conformation ring, commonly referred to as the breed ring, provides a forum for breeders and handlers to showcase the best in breeding stock. These animals are evaluated as potential breeding stock and are usually incorporated into future breeding programs in an effort to improve the breed. For this reason, dogs competing in conformation may not be spayed or neutered.

How Dog Shows Work

The best way to understand the conformation ring is to think of it in terms of an elimination process. Each Boston Terrier enters a regular class and is evaluated against the Boston Terrier breed standard. For the newcomer, it often appears as if the dogs are competing against one another. And, in a sense, they are. However, the judge is not comparing the quality of one Boston Terrier against the quality of another Boston Terrier. The judge is evaluating each Boston Terrier against the breed standard and how closely each dog measures up to the ideal Boston Terrier as outlined in the breed standard.

The regular classes are divided by sex with the male and female dogs judged separately. The male dogs are always judged first, and after being examined by the judge, they are placed first through fourth according to how well they measure up to the Boston Terrier breed standard in the judge's opinion. After the males have been judged, the females go through the same judging process.

After the regular classes have been judged, the first-place winners of each class are brought back to the ring to compete against one another in the Winners Class. The dog selected is the Winners Dog and is awarded championship points. A Reserve Winners Dog is also chosen but does not receive points unless the Winners Dog, for any reason, is disallowed or disqualified. The same process is then repeated with the female dogs, resulting in a Winners Bitch and Reserve Winners Bitch.

The Winners Dog and Winners Bitch go back into the ring, with any Champions entered, to compete for the Best of Breed award. If either the Winners Dog or Winners Bitch wins Best of Breed or Best of Winners, they may also win more points. The Best of Breed dog or bitch then goes on to the Group. The Group winners are then judged with Group placements—first through fourth place—being awarded in each of the seven groups. The first-place Group winners compete for the most coveted and most prestigious award: Best in Show.

Earning a Championship

To attain an AKC Championship title, each Boston Terrier must win a total of 15 points. Only the Winners Dog and Winners Bitch receive points. The number of points earned at each show is predetermined by a point schedule that varies from region to region.

The number of points awarded at each show depends on the breed, the number of dogs entered in the competition, and the location of the show. For example, points awarded to a Boston Terrier in New York will differ from the number of points awarded in California. The number of points that can be won at a show is between one and five. Three-, four, and five-point wins are considered *majors*. One- and two-point wins are considered *minors*. Of the 15 points required for a Championship title, six or more points must be majors. The remaining points may be attained in any combination, including major or minor wins, but must be won under different judges than the two major wins. So you need to win points under at least three different judges. A Boston can add to the number of points he won in the Winners Class if he also wins

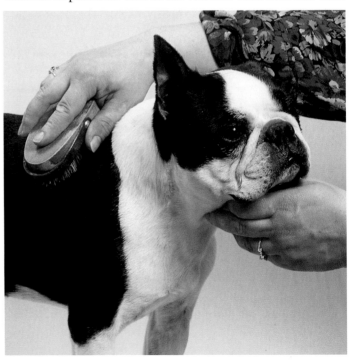

To compete in shows your dog must be in top condition and be groomed to perfection in order to look his best.

Best of Breed, Best of Opposite Sex, or Best of Winners. Once the requirements are met and officially confirmed, then a championship certificate is issued for the individual dog.

Canadian Kennel Club Championships

Winning a Championship title in Canada is slightly different. While the classes are basically the same, the CKC does not classify points as *majors* or *minors*. A Boston must win only 10 points to become a CKC Champion of Record. Of the 10 points required, the dog must win at least one two-point show at the breed or group level. The remaining points can be won in any combination.

OTHER FUN SPORTS

Walking, Jogging, and Hiking

Boston Terriers are always up for a romp in the park or a brisk walk or jog around the neighborhood. As a result, they make excellent exercise companions and, no doubt, both you and your Boston will benefit from the exercise and companionship. It is worth reiterating that Bostons cannot tolerate excessive temperatures, be they hot or cold. Therefore, if you plan to include your Boston in your daily walks or jogs, it is advisable to limit these activities to cooler parts of the day, such as the early morning or evening.

If you need to bundle up in a winter jacket or you're perspiring because of the heat, you might want to consider leaving your Boston at home. Be aware, too, that hot sidewalks and roads can burn a Boston's feet, causing an enormous amount of pain and discomfort. If the sidewalks and roadways are too hot for your bare feet, chances are they will be too hot for your Boston's feet.

Three Types of Dog Shows
- All-breed shows are exactly what the name implies. They are open to over 150 breeds and varieties of dogs recognized by the American Kennel Club, and include shows such as the prestigious Westminster Kennel Club. These are the types of conformation shows you are most likely to see on television.
- Specialty shows are for one specific breed, such as the Boston Terrier. Most often, local, regional, or national breed-specific clubs sponsor these shows.
- Group shows: shows that are limited to dogs belonging to one of the seven groups. For example, a Terrier-group show would feature only breeds belonging to the Terrier group.

Showing Your Dog

Dog showing is a gratifying and rewarding way to meet new people, spend countless hours with your Boston Terrier, and build a strong human/canine bond. However, dog showing, like most sports, must be learned and practiced regularly. If you are interested in conformation shows, you will need to learn to groom, condition, stack, and present your Boston Terrier in the best possible light. You will need to learn about the structure and movement of Boston Terriers. You will need to dress appropriately—not so flashy that you detract from your dog, but not so casual that you look like you came straight from mucking stalls. You will need proper shoes that provide comfort and are suitable for running. There are so many things of which you will have no control—the weather, judging schedules, bitches that come into season, schedules that move slower than you like—but you can control how you and your dog are represented and presented in the ring. Regardless of the event, you must have a thorough understanding and comprehension of the rules and regulations governing the show. You should obtain a copy of the rules and regulations for the governing organization, such as AKC, CKC, or UKC, and read through it several times. Most important, you must learn the art of winning and losing. Showing dogs requires a great deal of patience and objectivity. There will always be differences of opinion, shows you thought you should have won, and shows you won that you never should have. You must learn to be humble in your wins and gracious in your defeats.

The best way to get involved in showing dogs is to attend shows and ask a lot of questions. Most dog people are more than willing to help the newcomer. If possible, join a local dog club and find a mentor, such as a Boston Terrier breeder or professional handler, who is willing to help you navigate through the ins and outs of dog shows.

The distance your Boston can walk, jog, or hike, will depend on his age, physical condition, the terrain covered, and the weather. While a stroll around the block may be okay, an extended hike through rough terrain and rocky surfaces may be too taxing for some couch potatoes.

For the smaller Boston, you might want to consider a doggie backpack that you can tuck your precious pooch into should he become too tired. Also, it's always a good idea to carry plenty of fluid for both you and your Boston.

Swimming

Swimming is an excellent activity for cooling off, burning calories, and sharing quality time with your Boston Terrier. Be forewarned, not all Boston Terriers will take to the water. You may need to take it slowly and introduce your Boston to water playfully and gradually. It is never advisable to toss your Boston in the water. It's highly likely that doing so will frighten your Boston—not to mention possibly injure him and turn him off to swimming and water activities for the rest of his life.

For the reluctant Boston Terrier, try to find a swimming pool, lake, or shallow pond that has a gently sloping bank. Kiddy pools or wading pools are also excellent for the hesitant swimmer. Try to encourage your Boston to wade in with you or throw a floatable toy for him to retrieve, being careful in the beginning to toss it close to the bank of the pond or edge of the pool. If you toss it too far, it's likely he'll find the task of retrieving too daunting.

The ocean is wonderful for invigorating walks on the beach and dips in the ocean. Your Boston may be content to dip his feet in the foam, or he may be more adventurous and take a full body plunge. It is important to keep your Boston close to shore, regardless of his superior athleticism and swimming capabilities. Riptides and undercurrents are unpredictable, and your Boston could quickly wade into trouble.

Most dogs will play until they exhaust themselves and collapse into sleep. Therefore, it's important to watch for signs that your dog is getting tired, such as slowing down or slapping the water with his front feet. A lifejacket designed specifically for dogs may give you some peace of mind while providing a safety net for your water-loving companion.

Flyball

Invented in the late 1970s, Flyball is yet another exhilarating choice in the list of entertaining sports you can share with your Boston. To say Flyball is fast-paced is an understatement. It is a high-octane relay race that showcases a Boston's speed and agility. Don't worry—your Boston does all of the running in this sport! It's also an equally thrilling and entertaining spectator sport.

The course consists of four hurdles (small jumps) spaced approximately ten feet apart. Fifteen feet beyond the last hurdle is a spring-loaded box that contains a tennis ball. Just as in any relay race, the fastest team to successfully complete the game wins. The goal is for each dog to take a turn running the relay by leaping over each of the four hurdles and then hitting a pedal or lever with his paw to trigger the box, which shoots a tennis ball up in the air. Once the dog catches the ball, he races back over the four hurdles, where the next dog is waiting his turn.

The first team to have all four dogs run without errors wins the heat. If a dog misses a hurdle or fails to retrieve the ball, he must repeat his turn. The height of the hurdles is determined by the height of the shortest dog on the team, which could make your Boston Terrier quite the desired teammate. For additional information, contact the North American Flyball Association.

Canine Freestyle

Just when you think no one could possibly come up with yet another canine sport, along comes one! Canine Freestyle is an exciting and invigorating team sport that allows you and your Boston to kick up your heels, so to speak. In the simplest terms, Canine Freestyle is a choreographed performance between a dog and handler that is set to music.

Don't let the catchy name fool you. Canine freestyle is more than dogs heeling to music. The sport is patterned after Olympic skating with dogs and handlers performing twists, turns, leg kicks, pivots, and other cool and creative maneuvers. These maneuvers are entwined with basic obedience commands, such as heelwork, sit, down, and front. Many advanced competitors teach their dogs to crawl, back up, wave, bow, sidestep, bounce, rollover, spin, and play dead. Freestyle routines are varied and creatively choreographed with an emphasis on the special and unique bond that exists between a dog and handler. The fun is limited only by your imagination and creativity.

As with other canine sports, Canine Freestyle offers a number of divisions and categories to suit a dog and handler's varying levels of experience. Several organizations promote Canine Freestyle with styles varying between the organizations. For additional information, contact the Canine Freestyle Federation, Inc. (CFF) or the World Canine Freestyle Organization, Inc. (WCFO).

ASSISTANCE OR SERVICE DOGS

The terms *therapy dogs* and *service dogs* are often used interchangeably. However, there is a significant difference. The Americans with Disabilities Act uses the term s*ervice dog* to define a dog that has been "individually trained to work or perform tasks for the benefit of a person with a disability." Professionals within the industry often refer to them as assistance dogs, rather than service dogs. Therapy dogs provide companionship and emotional support. However, federal law does not legally define them. Under the umbrella of Assistance Dogs there are four categories: therapy dogs, guide dogs, service dogs, and hearing dogs.

THERAPY DOGS

Therapy is an important area in which Boston Terriers can help enhance the human/canine bond by providing unconditional love, companionship, and emotional support to nursing home, hospital, assisted-living, and mental-health residents. Owners volunteering with their Boston Terriers make regularly scheduled visits and brighten the lives of residents by providing stimulation, companionship, and a vehicle for conversation and interaction.

Bostons who are well-mannered and have a sound temperament make excellent candidates for therapy dogs.

HEALTH

Veterinary medicine has come a long way since melted goose-grease, strained through a sieve and mixed with spirits of wine and turpentine, was used as a dressing for wounds. Today, veterinary medicine is first-rate and, like good-quality nutrition, there is no substitute for regular veterinary care. There are any number of infectious diseases, parasites, and serious ailments that can impair your Boston's health, but today's veterinarians have the academic training and expertise necessary to reduce and prevent serious illnesses, helping to keep your Boston in the best health possible.

CHOOSING A VETERINARIAN

It is never too early to begin looking for a veterinarian. If your new Boston has yet to arrive at your home or you've recently moved, you will want to find a veterinarian before you actually need one. It is never a good idea to be scanning the yellow pages when your Boston is sick or injured. Just as you spent a great deal of time and energy finding the right Boston Terrier breeder, you will need to invest time and energy in finding a suitable veterinarian with whom you and your precious pooch will feel comfortable and can build a mutually trusting and respectful relationship.

Types of Veterinary Practices

There are a number of different veterinary practices, the most common being small-animal practices, where veterinarians work mainly with dogs and cats, and occasionally reptiles, ferrets, and birds. Oftentimes, these veterinarians will make house calls under special circumstances, such as to euthanize a sick or aging dog.

In rural areas, it is not unusual to see mixed-animal practices where veterinarians work with dogs and cats, as well as large animals including horses, llamas, cattle, goats, pigs, and other farm animals. Some veterinarians have mobile practices—a van or truck stocked with a variety of medical supplies—and, like doctors of years gone by, still make house calls and travel to your home or farm to treat your Boston.

Preparing for Emergencies

Anyone who has ever owned a dog knows that emergencies never happen between eight a.m. and five p.m. It's Murphy's Law with a twist. Anything that can go wrong will go wrong, and it will happen on weekends, holidays, and always after your veterinarian's office has just closed for the day. Therefore, it is always prudent to know the location of the closest emergency veterinary clinic. Emergency animal clinics can handle emergencies that occur outside of your veterinarian's regular office hours. Generally, they do not handle routine checkups, vaccinations, or spaying and neutering. Emergency clinics may also see animals that need 24-hour care or perform examinations with specialized equipment that other veterinarians may not have at their own facilities.

Veterinarians, Staff, and Assistants

Like human doctors, veterinarians differ in their bedside manners. No matter how qualified the veterinarian is, if you do not like him, her or the staff, you will not be comfortable taking your Boston there. The relationship between you and your veterinarian can last for many years. Good communication with the doctor and staff is a necessity.

- Are you comfortable talking with the veterinarian and asking questions?
- Does he or she seem knowledgeable and friendly?
- Is he or she patient? Willing to answer your questions? Responsive to your concerns?
- Does he or she explain the diagnosis, treatment, and expected outcome in layman's terms? Will that be explained again if you don't understand?
- Do you feel rushed?
- Is your Boston treated with kindness, respect, and concern?
- Is the staff knowledgeable, courteous, and friendly? Are they willing to answer your questions and accommodate reasonable requests or do they brush you off?

Of course, there is always the chance that you will not like a particular veterinarian despite his glowing recommendations and stellar academic qualifications. If this is the case, keep looking until you find the veterinarian that is right for you.

It's important to find a veterinarian you feel comfortable with and can trust; afterall, he'll have your dog's life in his hands.

PREVENTIVE CARE FOR YOUR BOSTON

Once you've found a veterinarian and you are happy and confident with your choice, it is time to get your Boston Terrier an appointment. Generally speaking, you will want to get your new pooch to the veterinarian within 48 to 72 hours after acquiring him. To the untrained eye, a puppy or adult dog can appear healthy, but may actually have a seri-

Visiting the Clinic

Visiting the clinic can be a bit time consuming, but, again, the time invested will be well worth the effort down the road. You may feel less anxious if you see where your Boston will be spending the day if he needs to be hospitalized overnight or kept for part of the day. When visiting veterinary clinics, don't be afraid to ask for a tour of their exam rooms, X-ray room, operating and recovery rooms, boarding areas, and so forth. If the clinic is busy or an emergency arises, you may need to schedule an appointment, which is not an unreasonable request. If the staff or veterinarians refuse to show you their facilities, run, don't walk, to the nearest exit.

When you're there, as about the regular office hours; how emergencies are handled; how long you need to wait for routine appointments; special services offered; whether the veterinarians there have experience with Boston Terriers; etc. Look to see if the clinic is neat, clean and organized; is there a place where the dogs can relieve themselves; does the waiting area accommodate enough people and their dogs?

ous problem. One of the most important and kindest deeds you can do for your Boston is to work with a veterinarian to develop a preventive healthcare plan and schedule routine visits.

The Physical Exam

Your veterinarian will check your Boston's overall condition, which includes inspecting his skin, coat, eyes, ears, feet, teeth and gums. He will listen to his heart and lungs, and feel his abdomen, muscle, and joints. Most likely, he will ask you about your puppy's eating and elimination habits. If necessary, jot down any relevant information before going to the vet's office so you will have it at your fingertips, such as the type of food your puppy eats, how much and how often he eats, how often he relieves himself, the color, shape, and size of his stool, and so forth. He will no doubt discuss with you a preventive healthcare plan that includes vaccinations, worming, spaying or neutering, and scheduling routine veterinary visits.

Annual Checkups

You may not feel older from one birthday to the next, but one year is a long time in a Boston Terrier's life. In a relatively short period of time, about seven years, your Boston will have grown from a tiny puppy to a senior citizen. In dog circles, a lot can happen in the span of one year, and that's why it is important to schedule (and keep!) annual checkups for your Boston. It's not unusual for owners to inadvertently overlook their Boston's health. Let's face it, how many people go to the doctor unless they're feeling particularly ill? When your Boston is happy and healthy and full of zest, annual preventive healthcare visits can get overlooked.

During an annual visit, your veterinarian will review important aspects of your dog's health, including:

- Your Boston's overall health, including weight, coat and skin condition, ears, eyes, feet, limbs, and respiratory functions.
- Nutritional requirements, including changes in appetite or water consumption, obesity, and special diets for aging Bostons.
- Exercise, including how often, what types, changes in your Boston's ability to exercise, walk, jog, etc.
- Vaccination requirements.
- Parasite control, including fleas, ticks, heartworms, and the like.
- Dental health, including mouth odors, pain, broken teeth, and related diseases.
- Blood tests for older dogs, those with medical conditions, and those receiving medications.
- Behavior changes in temperament and normal behaviors, problems with barking, chewing, digging, etc.
- Spaying or neutering.

Vaccinations

The sooner your Boston puppy starts his course of vaccinations, the sooner he will be able to get out and about and begin socializing with people and other animals and exploring his new world. A reputable breeder will most likely have administered a series of vaccinations for distemper, hepatitis, leptospirosis, parvovirus, and parain- fluenza prior to acquiring your Boston.

Vaccinations generally start being administered at six to eight weeks of age and continue every three to four weeks until the puppy is sixteen weeks old. You should have received a copy of his vaccination and deworming schedule when you picked up your Boston puppy. It is a good idea to take a copy of your puppy's vaccination schedule with you on your first visit to the veterinarian's office. Your veterinarian will set up a vaccination schedule for your Boston, including a rabies vaccination, at the appropriate time. Veterinarians differ on their vaccination protocol so it is important to ask questions, especially if you have any concerns.

Yearly checkups are especially important as your Boston ages. Older dogs are more likely to develop diabetes, kidney problems, and hormonal diseases—not to mention aches and pains and stiff joints. Yearly checkups will help your veterinarian to prevent diseases by catching them early on, keeping your Boston healthy well into his senior years.

COMMON HEALTH CONCERNS FOR BTs

The Boston Terrier is a fairly new breed—in the overall scheme of purebred dogs—and the breed remains relatively healthy. However, like most breeds, the Boston is not immune to hereditary health problems, and genetic diseases remain of paramount importance to reputable breeders. Certainly, the good health care you provide your Boston will help to influence and prolong his life. But sometimes, regard- less of your meticulous attention and best efforts, a Boston Terrier, for whatever reason, will develop a health problem.

To a large degree, your Boston's health is dictated by the genes he inherited from his ancestors, primarily his parents.

The Vaccination Controversy

Vaccination procedures have been under fire for quite some time, with some researchers advocating a not-so-traditional approach. The majority of experts agree that vaccinations are an important part of canine preventative medicine. They are also in agreement when it comes to puppy vaccinations, and the need to continue vaccinating all dogs for rabies. However, modern medicine and technology have helped scientists and researchers become more knowledgeable about vaccines, and canine medicine in general. As a result, many vaccines have improved and so, too, has the duration of immunity. Therein lies the controversy. Is it necessary to continue vaccinating dogs on a yearly basis? Simply put, are dogs being over-vaccinated, and what are the long-term health risks associated with this practice? Additionally, some researchers advocate rotating yearly vaccines using a single component vaccine—a vaccine, for example, that contains parvovirus—rather than combination vaccines that contain parvovirus, distemper, and hepatitis. A Boston would, for instance, receive a vaccination for disease A one year, and a vaccination for disease B the following year.

Modern medicine and technology will help keep your Boston happy and healthy, but the controversy surrounding vaccinations is not likely to fade anytime soon. No doubt, the future will bring many changes in traditional thinking as it pertains to vaccinations. We may even look back in astonishment at what was once viewed as a traditional and acceptable practice.

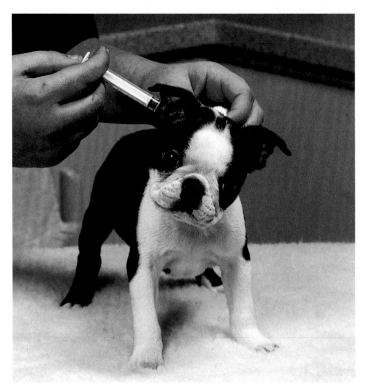

Your veterinarian will advise you about your puppy's necessary vaccinations to keep you on schedule.

He is the sum of his genetic makeup, which lays the foundation for his size, markings, structure, temperament, and overall health.

The genetic problems that are of primary concern to Boston Terrier breeders include atopic dermatitis, cataracts, deafness, and patellar luxation.

Atopic Dermatitis

When a Boston Terrier is allergic to a particular substance, his body reacts to certain molecules called allergens. Allergens are the substances that trigger an allergic reaction. Atopic dermatitis is an allergic skin condition caused by a hypersensitivity to environmental allergens that usually include house dust, dust mites, and molds. They can also include trees, grass, and weed pollens. The substances tend to be airborne allergens that are lightweight and move freely and easily through the air. Exposure to these allergens triggers an immune-system response that causes itchy, inflamed skin, which causes a dog to chew, scratch, and even bite at his skin.

AD usually occurs during the summer and fall seasons when pollen activity is high. The age of onset is usually between one and three years of age. Diagnosis is based on

There is no medical treatment available to prevent, reverse, or shrink cataracts. Surgery is the only known treatment, and newer, improved microsurgical techniques have increased the success rates of restoring vision to affected Boston Terriers.

clinical signs and a process of elimination, such as a skin scraping, to rule out parasites. The treatment for AD is very similar to flea allergy dermatitis—a strict flea-control program, hypoallergenic shampoos, topical anti-itch cream, and fatty acid supplements. A veterinarian may also prescribe corticosteroids for itching.

Cataracts

Cataracts are not uncommon in dogs. In fact, they are one of the more common problems affecting the eyes of dogs, and a leading cause of vision loss in dogs, including the Boston Terrier. However, the percentage of Boston Terriers overall with genetically inherited cataracts remains relatively low.

A normal, healthy lens is transparent. The term *cataract* is used to define an abnormality of the lens in which opacity causes the passage of light to the retina to become obstructed. The opacity often resembles a cloudy film on the surface of the eye, but, in fact, the opacity is deep inside your Boston's eyeball.

Cataracts are classified by several factors including the age of onset, specifically, the age of the dog at the time the cataract develops, and the cause. Congenital cataracts, for instance, mean they are present at birth. Congenital is frequently confused with inherited, but the two terms are completely different. Most cataracts are inherited, but non-hereditary cataracts can also occur as a result of trauma or other diseases, such as diabetes.

The most common cataracts in Boston Terriers are juvenile cataracts. Remember, juvenile simply refers to the age at which the cataract develops, which in the Boston breed generally means up to about four years of age. These types of cataracts may progress to blindness or they may remain small and not impair a Boston's vision at all.

Cataracts are also classified by their location, and the degree of opacity. Cataracts can assume a variety of appearances depending on the severity of the situation. They can appear as small white flecks in the eye, which may not cause any visual impairment. In more severe cases, where the opacity is nearly compete and the eye takes on a milky white haze or cloudy appearance, vision loss may range from partial to complete blindness.

Your veterinarian may be able to confirm the presence of mature or complete cataracts, but small cataracts are usually found by first dilating the dog's pupil and then examining the lens with high-tech equipment found in veterinary ophthalmology clinics.

It is worth noting that cataracts differ from nuclear sclerosis, which is a normal change that occurs in the lens of older dogs. It is the slight graying of the lens that owners frequently mistake for cataracts. It usually occurs in both eyes at the same time and occurs in most dogs over the age of six.

Deafness

Like humans, dogs can have hearing problems. Hearing loss can range from mild to complete deafness, which can present unique and challenging problems, not to mention frustration and heartache, for both owners and breeders. Unilaterally deaf dogs—dogs that have only a partial hearing loss or deafness in one ear—can make excellent pets with only minor adjustments in the dog's lifestyle and living conditions. They may take a bit more time and patience

The Boston is a relatively healthy breed overall, and you can keep your dog that way with proper care.

to train, but they can and do learn to adapt and live otherwise normal, happy lives. Bilaterally deaf dogs—dogs that are deaf in both ears—present the most challenges.

There are two types of deafness: congenital and acquired. If a Boston has normal hearing at several months of age, he will continue to have hearing unless something goes awry, such as trauma or infection. This falls under the category of acquired deafness.

Congenital deafness, deafness that is present at birth, is reported in approximately 60 breeds and is the primary form of deafness in the Boston Terrier breed. This type of deafness is thought to be caused by the genes that are responsible for producing white markings and blue eyes.

If your Boston has any white in his coat, he almost certainly has one of the versions of the piebald gene—the gene that causes the white over-markings. The piebald gene pro-

BAER Testing

Most veterinarians can make an elementary diagnosis of bilateral deafness through behavior testing. However, an electrodiagnostic test called a BAER (Brainserm Auditory Evoked Response) will provide definitive results, and is the only way a unilaterally deaf dog can be tested. The testing is done by placing extremely tiny electrodes under the scalp on a dog's head and measuring the electric impulse produced, not unlike an antenna that detects radio or television signals. Testing can be done as early as six weeks of age, and sedation is normally not necessary.

duces irregular, nonsymmetrical patterns of white, half-white heads, white heads, and excessively wide white collars. Experts believe that the amount of white on the dog's head appears to share a close relationship to deafness in Boston Terriers, as well as other breeds.

The inner ear contains a tiny organ called a cochlea, which, if you remember from biology class, is shaped like a snail's shell. It contains a fluid that is lined with tiny hair-like cells and is responsible for translating the mechanical vibration that is a sound wave into electrical impulses that can travel via nerves to the brain. This process is called transduction. Here's a simplified version of how it works: vibrations travel through the ear canal and vibrate the fluid within the cochlea. These vibrations wiggle the hair-like cells that connect the nerve endings to the brain.

The pigment cells play an important role in connecting each hair-like cell to its corresponding nerve. If pigment cells fail to reach the inner ear, the lack of pigment cells will cause the hair-like cells to die off about three weeks after a puppy is born. Without the hair-like cells, sound can't be transmitted and the result is deafness. Bostons with considerable amounts of white on or immediately surrounding the ear are more likely to also be lacking pigment within the ear. The more pigment cells that are missing, the greater the hearing loss.

To further complicate the matter, some Boston Terriers with perfectly acceptable markings and two dark eyes (as opposed to blue eyes) are bilaterally deaf. Experts believe defective genes, genes other than those involved in the piebald gene, may be responsible, and those genes may be inherited differently. Unfortunately, no one knows for certain what the causes are.

Patellar Luxation

Patellar luxation is a medical term used to describe a slipped or dislocated kneecap--*Patella* meaning *kneecap*, and *luxating* meaning *a joint that is abnormally out of place*. The problem is a concern for breeders of Boston Terriers, as well as other small and toy breeds.

There are three major components involved in luxating patellas: the femur (thigh bone), patella (knee cap), and tibia (second thigh). The three components come together at the stifle, the anatomical equivalent of the human knee. A Boston's kneecap, which is very similar to a human's kneecap, is the flat, moveable bone at the front of the knee. Its job is to protect the large tendon of the quadriceps muscles used to straighten the stifle.

Here's how they come together: In a normal knee, the femur and tibia are lined up so the patella can slide up and down in a groove on the face of the lower end of the femur. The patella ligament and the attached muscles hold the patella in place while the sliding motion allows the dog to bend or straighten his leg. All the pieces fit together in a predefined way. If you place your hand on your kneecap while bending and straightening your knee, you will feel the normal movement of the knee as it glides up and down in the groove.

Here are things that can go wrong that may result in a luxated patella: The groove is shallow and not well developed, or the femur and tibia are not properly lined up so the patella rests securely in the groove. In these instances, there is little to prevent the kneecap from shifting or slipping out of place and riding on the inner surface of the femur. In addition, the lack of stability of the patellar tendon can cause the kneecap to slip out of place. Any of these conditions, or a combination of them, can result in a dislocated kneecap.

Patellar luxations are a congenital condition, meaning the structural changes that lead to

Diagnosis of patellar
luxation is relatively simple
and can be done by a
veterinarian who is familiar
with orthopedics. In most
cases, it entails a physical
examination that includes
palpation of the joint and
manual luxation of the
kneecap when the puppy is
around four to six months
of age.

luxation are present at the time of birth. The actual disloca-
tion may not be present, but the writing is on the wall, so to
speak. In addition, luxated patellas are thought to be inherited, but the exact mode of inheritance—the genes that
cause the abnormality—is not yet known.

Patellar luxation is graded according to severity:

- Grade 1: This is the least severe condition. When pal-
  pated by a veterinarian, the kneecap slips out of the
  groove when the knee is fully extended, but returns to
  the groove when released.
- Grade 2: The kneecap tends to dislocate more frequently, and tends to stay luxated for longer periods of
  time, which, in some cases, can lead to irreversible
  damage.
- Grade 3: The patella is permanently luxated, but can be
  replaced manually. A Boston will use the leg, but without full extension.
- Grade 4: This is the most severe condition. The patella
  is stuck in a dislocated position and cannot be replaced
  manually. Extension of the knee is nearly impossible,
  with most Bostons having a bow-legged appearance.

Surgical correction to correct the alignment is frequently the recommended treatment, coupled with a weight management program to keep extra pounds from exacerbating the problem.

PROTECTING AGAINST HEAT

Heatstroke, also known as hyperthermia, is not a genetically inherited disease. However, being a brachycephalic breed, the Boston Terrier is at a higher risk for heatstroke than non-brachycephalic breeds because of their compromised ability to cool themselves. As a result, a Boston Terrier is more likely to be subjected to a moderate or severe case of heatstroke in a shorter period of time than, say, an Australian Shepherd or Border Collie. Equally important, overweight Bostons, puppies, and older Bostons are more vulnerable to heat-induced illnesses than Boston Terriers in good physical condition and otherwise excellent health.

Heat-induced illnesses occur when a dog's normal body mechanisms cannot keep his temperature within a safe range. Unlike humans, dogs do not sweat. Their primary cooling mechanisms are evaporation and conduction. Evaporation occurs when a dog pants and water is lost through the moist mucous membranes of the upper respi-

When there is a compromised airway, as in Boston Terriers and other brachycephalic breeds, the normal cooling process becomes a bit of a vicious cycle, because the increased panting can cause further swelling and narrowing of the dog's already constricted airways, which causes an increase in the dog's anxiety. As a result, evaporation is reduced, which further impairs breathing and increases the need for respiration.

ratory tract. This is an efficient method of cooling, but the act of panting also generates heat. In most dogs, this does not present significant problems.

Conduction, the second method of cooling, occurs when a dog lies down on a cool surface, such as a tile floor, grass, or wet concrete. The heat is transferred to the cool surface.

There are four types of heat-induced illnesses: heat cramps, heat exhaustion, heat prostration, and heatstroke. Heat cramps are muscle cramps that are caused by the loss of salt from a dog's system, and by extreme exertion in hot weather. Heat cramps don't normally occur in dogs, and it's highly unlikely you will encounter them in a Boston Terrier. The specific heat-related health issues that you should be aware of are heat exhaustion, heat prostration, and heatstroke.

Heat Exhaustion

Heat exhaustion is the least severe of the heat-related illnesses. However, it should still be taken seriously. It is often referred to as a *mild* case of heatstroke, and is characterized by lethargy and an inability to perform normal activities or work, such as obedience, agility, or tracking, because of extreme heat.

Heat Prostration

On the continuum of heat-induced illnesses, heat prostration is the next level. It would be considered a *moderate* case of heatstroke with a dog's body temperature around 104 to 106 degrees. Possible signs would include rapid panting, red or pale gums, weakness, vomiting, mental confusion, and dizziness. You should not delay in seeking immediate veterinary attention. Dogs with a moderate case of heatstroke can often recover without complicating health problems.

Heatstroke

Heatstroke is the more severe form of heat prostration and occurs when a dog's body temperature is over 106 degrees. Dogs suffering from heatstroke will display symptoms that include rapid panting, inability to stand up, red or pale gums, thick and sticky saliva, weakness, vomiting (with or without blood), diarrhea, shock, fainting, or a coma. At this stage, it is a life-threatening medical emergency that can result in multiple organ system dysfunction, including the respiratory, cardiovascular, gastrointestinal, renal, and central nervous systems. Immediate veterinary assistance is essential.

What Should You Do?

Get your dog to a cool environment immediately. Lower his temperature by submerging his body in cool (not cold) water—keeping his head elevated above the water—or applying cool water to his body with a shower or hose. If he will drink on his own, give him water or a rehydrating solution. Don't force water down his gullet, as he's likely to choke. Place him on a wet towel to keep him cool, and seek medical assistance immediately.

If your Boston becomes overheated, lower his body temperature gradually by bathing in cool—not cold—water or applying cool, wet towels.

VIRAL AND BACTERIAL DISEASES

Distemper

Distemper is a highly contagious viral disease that is very similar to the virus that causes measles in humans. It can spread rapidly through kennels or multiple-dog households, especially if unvaccinated dogs are present. Distemper is spread through the air as well as through contact with an infected animal's stool or urine. It is a primary cause of illness and death in unvaccinated puppies.

Dogs of any age can be affected; however, most are puppies less than six months of age. Distemper attacks a wide range of canine organs including the skin, brain, eyes, respiratory, digestive, and nervous systems. Symptoms usually appear about 10 to 14 days after exposure. A Boston Terrier with distemper may develop nasal and eye discharge, coughing, diarrhea, vomiting, and seizures. Puppies that recover may develop severe enamel damage on their teeth, retinal damage, seizures, and muscular twitches. They may also have nose and footpads that become thickened, hence the nickname *hardpad* disease.

Hepatitis

Hepatitis, also known as canine adenovirus, typically affects the liver, tonsils, and larynx, but can also attack other organs in the body. Initial symptoms include a sore throat, coughing, and occasionally pneumonia. As it enters a Boston's bloodstream, it can affect the liver, kidneys, and the appearance of the eyes, which may become cloudy or bluish. More advanced symptoms are characterized by seizures, increased thirst, vomiting, and diarrhea. The virus is spread primarily through direct contact with an infected dog and infected fluids, including saliva, nasal discharge, and urine. Bostons that were infected but have since recovered can still pass the virus for up to nine months in their urine. Unvaccinated Boston Terriers of all ages are at risk. However, the disease is most prevalent in dogs less than one year of age.

Leptospirosis

Leptospirosis is a bacterial disease that is transmitted primarily through the urine of infected animals. The disease can get into water or soil and can survive for weeks to months. Boston Terriers, as well as humans, can become infected through contact with the contaminated urine or the contaminated water or soil. A Boston that drinks, swims, or walks through contaminated water can also become infected. Symptoms can include fever, vomiting, abdominal pain, diarrhea, loss of appetite, weakness, lethargy, stiffness, severe muscle pain, and even death.

Parvovirus

Parvo is a highly contagious gastrointestinal disease that normally affects puppies more frequently than adult dogs. The majority of puppies infected are under six months of age, with the most severe cases seen in puppies younger than 12 weeks of age. The virus, which is spread through the stools of infected dogs, is resistant to environmental influences, such as heat and cold, and can survive on clothes, dog bowls, and kennel floors for five months—or longer in the right conditions. The normal incubation period—the time period between exposure to the virus and the time when symptoms begin to appear—can be as short as four days after exposure. Symptoms include vomiting, diarrhea (often times dark and bloody), fever, and dehydration. In very young puppies, parvovirus can also affect the heart muscle, which can lead to death within a matter of hours.

Kennel Cough

Kennel cough, also known as canine infectious tracheo-bronchitis or Bordetellosis, results from an inflammation of a dog's upper airways. Highly contagious, the respiratory disease is normally characterized by harsh, dry coughing or hacking, which may be followed by retching and gagging. The disease is airborne—meaning it is passed through the air—and can spread rapidly among dogs that live together. Boston Terriers at shows, boarding kennels, grooming shops, veterinary clinics, and public or private dog parks are at an increased risk to exposure. While kennel cough is a serious problem, it isn't normally fatal unless a secondary infection, such as pneumonia, develops. In severe infections, discharges from the nose and mouth occur along with depression, lack of energy, and loss of appetite.

Rabies

All warm-blooded animals—including humans—are at risk for contracting rabies. Rabies is a viral disease that affects the brain and is almost invariably fatal once symptoms begin to appear. Transmission of the virus is almost always through a bite from a rabid animal. The virus is relatively slow moving with the average incubation time from exposure to brain involvement (in dogs) being between three and eight weeks, though it can be as long as six months.

Clinical symptoms vary within the different stages of rabies. If you suspect your Boston Terrier has been bitten by a wild animal or infected dog or cat, it is always best to err on the side of caution and seek veterinary assistance immediately. There is no cure for rabies. However, vaccination is the best way to prevent infection, and properly vaccinated animals are at a relatively low risk of contracting the disease.

Lyme Disease

Lyme disease was first diagnosed in 1975 in Lyme, Connecticut, yet there is evidence that it existed in wildlife for many, many years prior. Lyme disease, a bacterial infection caused by a slender spiral microorganism identified as *Borrelia burgdorferi,* is transmitted to humans and dogs

Dogs who come into contact with many different dogs in different kinds of places should be vaccinated against kennel cough.

through the bite of an infected deer tick, also known as the black-legged tick. Cases of Lyme disease are most prevalent in the northeastern, mid-Atlantic, and north central states. Illness may not show up for months after initial exposure to an infected tick, and the severity of the disease may vary depending on the dog's age and immune status.

The most common symptoms are a fever of between 103 and 105 degrees, shifting leg lameness, swelling in the joints, and lethargy. Treatment usually involves an oral antibiotic prescription, but Lyme disease can be difficult to cure because the symptoms reoccur. Occasionally, it develops into a chronic state—becoming a "waxing and waning" illness in which the symptoms come and go.

PROTOZOAL INTESTINAL INFECTIONS

Protozoa are one-celled organisms or parasites that infect the intestinal tract of dogs. Two of the most common protozoal infections that affect Boston Terriers are giardiasis and coccidiosis.

Giardia

Giardia, pronounced *GEE-are-DEE-uh*, live in the small intestine of dogs. Infection with Giardia is called giardiasis. The microscopic parasites reproduce by dividing in two and then, after an unknown number of divisions, they are passed

in the stool. It has been nicknamed the backpackers' disease, because it is commonly acquired by drinking infected water in high mountain lakes and streams. Beavers are most often blamed for contaminating the water by passing the intestinal organism in their feces. However, Giardia can also be tracked into your house or kennel from your shoes or boots.

Dogs who spend any time outside need to be checked for ticks.

Giardia prevents proper absorption of nutrients, damages the intestinal lining, and interferes with digestion. In many cases involving adult dogs, there are few symptoms associated with giardiasis. Younger dogs may develop diarrhea or abnormal, soft, or light-colored stools that have a bad odor and greasy appearance. Some dogs will not lose their appetite, but they may lose weight.

Thanks to the marvels of modern technology, new tests make Giardiasis easier to diagnosis, which, of course, allows veterinarians to begin treating the problem much earlier. Veterinarians differ in their treatment because there are currently no drugs approved for treating giardiasis in dogs. Oftentimes, treatment is given to control secondary infection.

Coccidia

Coccidia invade the cells of the small intestine where they

multiply rapidly and destroy tissue. They are most common in puppies less than six months of age and in adult dogs with suppressed immune systems. They are also found in dogs that are under physiological stress, such as change of ownership, shipping, weaning, overcrowding, fatigue, dietary changes, or when other diseases are present.

As puppies age, they tend to develop a natural immunity to the effects of coccidia. An adult dog may carry coccidia in his intestines and shed the parasites in his feces, yet show no symptoms or experience any ill effects. A young Boston Terrier may experience diarrhea streaked with blood, weight loss, diminished appetite, and, in some instances, even death.

Coccidia is spread in the feces of carrier animals. Once infected, the disease is referred to as coccidiosis. Puppies are not born with the organisms in their body, but they may be exposed to the feces of their mother or to the environment. If she is shedding the infective parasites in her feces, then the young puppies will likely ingest them and coccidia will develop in their intestines. This is by far the most common mode of infection in young dogs. However, puppies can be infected or reinfected when they groom themselves or their siblings. Cockroaches and flies can also carry coccidia from one location to another, and a Boston Terrier that eats mice or other animals infected with coccidia can also become infected.

Coccidiosis is highly contagious, and any infected puppy is contagious to other puppies. Therefore, to control the spread of coccidiosis, it is important to practice strict sanitation practices. Fecal matter should be removed daily and water and food should be housed so that it cannot become contaminated with feces.

Fortunately, coccidiosis is treatable with prescription drugs. The drugs do not kill the organisms but instead inhibit their reproduction capabilities.

WORMS (INTERNAL PARASITES)

Parasites. They sound grotesque, and to the average dog owner, they usually are. Unfortunately, it is highly likely that sometime within your Boston's life he will acquire a case of worms, and you will have to deal with it.

Internal parasites are called *endoparasites* (*endo* means

Think of internal parasites as unwanted freeloading relatives or friends. They find a secret place inside your Boston Terrier where they live, steal food, deposit their offspring, and then leave to find another unsuspecting Boston Terrier, where they repeat the freeloading process.

in), meaning they live inside your Boston Terrier's body. The most common are roundworms, hookworms, tapeworms, and whipworms. Heartworms live internally and are potentially the most dangerous parasite. Have a veterinarian diagnose the specific type of internal parasite and then prescribe the proper deworming medication.

Pups may inherit internal parasites from their mothers at birth, but they are easily cured of them.

Roundworms

Roundworms, often called *ascarids,* are one of the most common parasites of the canine digestive tract. They live in the small intestine of your Boston Terrier and are usually three to four inches long, but can be up to seven inches long. They are round, hence their catchy name, and tend to look quite a bit like spaghetti.

Most puppies are born with roundworms even if a breeder maintains exceptional sanitary whelping conditions. This is why most puppies require deworming at an early age. A pregnant bitch that has roundworms can pass them to her puppies in two ways. The larvae that were dormant in her tissues can migrate through the uterus and placenta and into the lungs of the unborn puppy. When the puppy is born, it coughs up the larvae and then swallows them, where they mature in the puppy's intestines. Puppies can also become infected through ingestion of their mother's milk.

Dogs can also ingest roundworms when they eat an

infected animal, such as a rodent, or when they ingest soil contaminated with roundworms. Bostons that like to snack from the cat's litter box can eat infected feces where the roundworm eggs pass through the dog's digestive system.

Roundworms can cause serious problems for dogs and huge headaches for owners.

When they infect your Boston's intestines, they absorb nutrients, interfere with digestion, and can damage the lining of the intestine. In more severe infestations, dogs may be thin and have a potbellied appearance. Their coats may be dry, dull, and rough-looking. Some puppies may have intestinal discomfort and may cry as a result. Diarrhea or constipation and vomiting are also frequent symptoms. In some cases, a cough may develop due to the migration of the larvae through the respiratory system.

Roundworms are resistant to environmental conditions and most common disinfectants. They can adhere to fur, skin, and paws, so good hygiene and strict sanitation are important to minimize further contamination. Feces should be picked up on a daily basis. Once roundworms get into your soil, they can live for months or years. Tilling the soil to a depth of 8 to 12 inches, removing it, and replacing it with new soil, or paving the entire area is about the only way to totally solve the problem.

Hookworms

Hookworms are another common internal parasite of dogs—especially puppies. They are only about one-half inch long, but they can cause serious health problems for your Boston Terrier, including diarrhea, vomiting, and life-threatening anemia. A Boston's gums may appear pale, the dog may be weak, and sometimes black, tarry stools can be seen. In severe cases, a blood transfusion may be necessary.

The adult hookworms have teeth-like structures or *hooks* that attach to the lining of your Boston's intestine and feed on his oxygen-carrying blood. Adult hookworms then lay eggs that are passed in the dog's feces, where they hatch into larvae. Thus the cycle of infestation continues.

A Boston can become infected when larvae enter through the skin and migrate through the bloodstream to the lungs and trachea. The larvae are then coughed up and swallowed, where they attach themselves to the intestinal wall.

Ingesting contaminated food or water, licking his contaminated feet, or ingesting an infected host can also infect a Boston. Most ingested larvae pass directly down to the intestine, where they remain.

A puppy can become infected when larvae migrate to the uterus or mammary glands of a pregnant bitch, thereby infecting the fetuses or nursing puppies.

Hookworms can also be contracted either through a dog's mother or through contaminated soil and feces, which makes sanitary practices extremely important. All fecal material should be removed daily. When walking in public places, do not allow your dog to come in contact with other dogs' feces.

Tapeworms

Tapeworms are another common internal parasite found in dogs. While generally not life-threatening, they are definitely a problem. Unlike the whipworms, roundworms, and hookworms, tapeworms must go through an intermediate host in order for larvae to develop. In dogs, the most common hosts are fleas and lice, which ingest the eggs and subsequently set up housekeeping for the larvae.

When your Boston Terrier ingests the flea or lice, it ingests the resident tapeworm. In certain species of tapeworms, rabbits and livestock can be the intermediate hosts. While less common, infections can occur when dogs eat or scavenge the internal body parts of wild game or the discarded parts of butchered livestock, or are given raw meat.

Tapeworms are flat and can be several feet long. They are segmented and consist of a head, neck, and then a number of segments, which contain large numbers of eggs that break away from the rest of the worm and are passed in the feces. The head usually has suckers or muscular grooves that enable the tapeworm to attach itself to your Boston's intestine.

Tapeworms generally do not cause any symptoms, although diarrhea may be present. In severe infestations, your Boston may exhibit abdominal discomfort or nervousness. The dog may vomit and in some cases experience convulsions, which are thought to be caused from the toxins produced by the tapeworm. The tiny segments, which look like tiny grains of uncooked rice, are passed through the feces. They are sometimes visible on the dog's rectum or in his stool. Some dogs will scoot their rear ends along the ground.

Getting rid of tapeworms can be difficult because you must successfully eliminate the head of the tapeworm, otherwise it will regrow a new body. Flea and lice control are essential, otherwise your Boston will continue to be reinfested.

Whipworms

Whipworms get their name from the whiplike shape of the adult worm. Dogs become infected when they ingest food or water that is contaminated with whipworm eggs. The eggs are swallowed, hatch in the large intestine, and in about three months the larvae mature into adults that attach to the intestinal lining and burrow their mouths into the intestinal wall, where they feed on blood. Adult worms lay eggs that are passed in the feces.

The symptoms vary depending on the number of worms in a dog's stomach. Oftentimes, mild infestations produce no obvious symptoms in healthy individuals. Larger infestations, however, have more pronounced symptoms and can result in inflammation of the intestinal wall. Anemia is possible if hemorrhaging into the intestine occurs. Some dogs may experience diarrhea, mucus and blood in the stools, and loss of weight.

Whipworms can live in moist soil for years and are resistant to freezing. However, dry conditions, good drainage, sunlight, and aeration of kennels, dog runs, and exercise areas will destroy whipworm eggs. Like roundworms, soil contamination is an enormous problem. To help reduce or prevent contamination, fecal matter should be picked up daily and kennel or dog-run areas cleaned thoroughly. If possible, dog runs should dry in direct sunlight.

Keep track of your dog's worming, flea, and vaccination schedule on a calendar or journal that you look at frequently. Write down the dates he was treated, and then flip ahead and jot down the dates he's due for another treatment. Not all veterinarians send reminders, and more than a few get lost in the mail.

Heartworms

Heartworms are potentially the most dangerous internal parasite and are found throughout the United States. Mosquitoes transmit the disease when they suck blood from an infected dog and then bite a healthy dog, thereby depositing larvae. The larvae grow inside the healthy dog, passing through the dog's tissues into the bloodstream and eventually into the dog's heart. The larvae grow into adult worms between 6 and 14 inches in length. The process is relatively slow and can take about six to seven months from the time the dog is bitten until an adult heartworm develops. A severely infected dog can have several hundred heartworms in his heart and vessels. The worms can completely fill and obstruct the heart chambers and the various large blood vessels leading from the heart to the lungs.

Dogs with heartworm infections may not show symptoms until the damage is extensive and the disease is well

advanced. A chronic cough is often the first symptom followed by a decrease in appetite, loss of weight, listlessness, and fatigue after light exercise. Some dogs accumulate fluid in their abdomens and take on a potbellied appearance. In rare situations, the dog may die of sudden heart failure.

Diagnosis is usually done with a blood test that detects adult antigens in the blood. Heartworm treatment is not without risk because some—but not all—of the drugs used to kill the adult worms contain arsenic. The death of the worms can also create blood clots in a dog, which also presents life-threatening problems. The protocol your veterinarian chooses will depend on the severity of infection, and whether or not your Boston's kidneys and liver can tolerate the treatment.

Preventive medications are available and are highly recommended. However, they must never be given to a dog that is already infected with adult worms. Therefore, it is imperative that you consult with your veterinarian before starting any preventative treatment for heartworms.

Heartworm preventive, given regularly to even young dogs, will keep them safe from this terrible disease.

EXTERNAL PARASITES

Fleas

If you own a Boston Terrier, you no doubt know a thing or two about fleas. One bite from these pesky creatures can cause itching for days. And where there's one flea, it's a safe bet there are plenty more in your carpet, furniture, bedding, and on your Boston. What you may not know is that there are over 2,200 species of fleas worldwide.

In North America, only a few species of fleas commonly infest dogs. The *Ctenocephalides felis*, also known as the domestic cat flea, likes both cats and dogs, and is the most common flea responsible for wreaking havoc with your Boston Terrier. They are about one-eighth-inch long, slightly smaller than a sesame seed, and generally brown or black in color. These wingless bloodsuckers are responsible for spreading tapeworms to dogs and causing serious allergy dermatitis, and in serious infestations, fleas can cause anemia, especially in puppies.

The Flea's Life Cycle

There are four stages in the development of fleas: eggs, larvae, pupae (cocoon), and adults. Why is this important, you ask? To effectively eliminate fleas—or at least get and keep the upper hand—it is helpful to understand the life cycle of fleas. Male and females mate, and two days later (yes, two days!) the females start laying eggs. Females average about 27 eggs a day, but can produce up to 40 or 50 eggs per day during peak egg production. The entire life cycle of the cat flea can be completed in as little as 12 to 14 days. If you do the math, 25 adult female fleas can multiply to as many as 250,000 fleas in just 30 days. The eggs are frequently deposited on your Boston Terrier and readily fall off into the environment, including carpets and rugs, furniture, soil, shrubbery, and your dog's bedding.

The female also deposits a large amount of feces, often called *flea dirt*, which is the reddish-brown residue frequently found on your Boston Terrier when he has fleas. It is primarily dried blood that is passed in the feces of adult fleas.

Somewhere between one and six days after being laid, the eggs begin to hatch into wormlike larvae that feed on the

Itchy Skin

Skin problems are a real pain—literally and figuratively! They can range from mild to severe, and can be quite challenging to identify, manage, or eliminate. The more common dermatologic conditions seen in dogs, including Boston Terriers, are flea allergy dermatitis, atopic dermatitis, and demodectic mange.

feces (flea dirt) left by its mother. The larvae pass through several different development stages, and a week or two later they begin spinning a cocoon in which they transform from larvae into pupae—the nonfeeding stage between the larvae and adult stage. About a week later, the pupae develop into adult fleas that begin searching for a host.

Getting Rid of Fleas

The first step in eliminating fleas from your Boston is to prevent them from coming into contract with him. This entails a thorough cleaning, both inside and out. You need to get the adult fleas, eggs, larvae, and pupae out of your house, your dog's house and bed, and all the areas that your Boston frequents, including your automobiles and yard. Wash his dog beds and blankets and mop the floors. Vacuum all carpets, rugs, and furniture. Immediately dispose of vacuum bags because eggs can hatch in them.

If necessary, dense vegetation near your home, dog yard, or kennel area may need to be removed, as these spaces offer a damp microenvironment that is favorable to flea development. Leaves and other organic debris should be removed to allow the soil to dry. Opening these areas to sunlight will reduce environments that are conducive to fleas.

Cat fleas that are living on your Boston do not leave unless forced off by grooming activity or insecticides. Therefore, in addition to ridding your environment of fleas, you will need to simultaneously treat your Boston and any other household pets that can serve as hosts, such as other dogs, cats, and ferrets.

A number of insecticides and insect-growth regulators are available for use in the home and have proven effective. However, it is worth noting that some insecticides are toxic. It is important to read all labels and follow directions carefully. There are also a number of on-animal flea-control products, such as shampoos, sprays, dips, powders, and flea collars. Many of these products have been around for years,

Eradicating fleas is easier said than done. Pupae can remain dormant in the cocoon for up to six months, which is important to remember when planning flea control. If you live where the temperature freezes, count your blessings. The cat flea is susceptible to cold, and no life stage of the flea can survive when exposed to temperatures below 3 degrees Celsius, or roughly 37 degrees Fahrenheit.

but, again, it is important to remember that many commercial and natural products may be toxic. They may irritate your Boston's skin or cause health problems. Equally important, they are most effective when used in conjunction with a rigorous flea-control program. A flea collar alone will not provide your Boston with a flea-free environment.

The advent of once-a-month squeeze-on products has made flea control much easier and effective than in the past. Your veterinarian can assist you in choosing the right flea-control products for your four-legged friend.

Flea Allergy Dermatitis (FAD)

If your Boston is sensitive to fleas, one bite from this tiny, nearly invisible pest can make his life miserable and plunge him into a vicious cycle of biting, scratching, and licking. Flea allergy dermatitis, also known as bite hypersensitivity, tends to be most prevalent during the summer when fleas are most rampant and annoying.

Fleas feeding on your Boston Terrier inject saliva that contains different antigens and histamine-like substances, resulting in irritation and itching sensations that can range from mild to severe. Dogs with flea allergies may itch over their entire bodies, experience generalized hair loss, and develop red, inflamed skin and hot spots. They are frequently restless and uncomfortable, and may spend a great deal of their time scratching, digging, licking, and chewing at their skin.

Treatments vary and can be multifaceted. Of primary importance is a strict flea-control program to prevent additional infestation. Veterinarians frequently recommend hypoallergenic or colloidal oatmeal-type shampoos to remove allergens, and topical anti-itch creams to soothe the skin. These products usually provide immediate, short-term relief, but are not a long-term solution. Additionally, fatty acid supplements, such as Omega-3 and Omega-6, are proving helpful in reducing the amount and effects of histamine. In some cases, veterinarians may prescribe corticosteroids to reduce itching.

Ticks

Unlike fleas, which are insects and have six legs, ticks, like mites and spiders, are arachnids and have eight legs. There are approximately 850 species of these blood-sucking para-

If possible, avoiding tick-infested areas during the peak tick season will help. When taking your Boston for a walk, do not allow him to wander off designated paths or near overhanging branches and shrubs where there are likely to be ticks. Your local university or health department should be able to provide you with information on the types of ticks found in your area, and their peak seasons.

sites that burrow into your Boston's skin and engorge themselves with blood, expanding to many times their size. They
are dangerous because they can secrete a paralysis-causing
toxin and can spread serious diseases such as Lyme disease,
Rocky Mountain spotted fever, Texas fever, tularemia,
babesiosis, and canine ehrlichiosis. It is not unusual for a
tick to be infected with and transmit more than one disease.
Therefore, it is not at all uncommon to see a dog infected
with more than one disease at a time. In severe infestations,
anemia and even death may occur

Your Boston is likely to pick up ticks in wooded areas,
grassy areas, and overgrown fields. Ticks commonly imbed
themselves between the toes, in the ears, and around the
neck but can be found elsewhere on the body. Each species
has their own favored feeding sites on your Boston Terrier.

Controlling ticks on your Boston is not unlike the
process for flea control. You must be committed, and you
must be diligent. You will want to treat your yard, house,

Your Boston can pick up ticks almost anywhere outside. Always go over him thoroughly after walks or other outdoor activities.

doghouse, dog blankets, and your dog, with a product specifically designed for ticks. There are a number of over-the-counter products available, such as sprays, foggers, powders, dips, shampoos, and collars. Unlike fleas, ticks are not susceptible to cold weather, so you will need to treat your yard late into the fall and early winter. Again, many of these products may be toxic. It is important to read all labels and follow directions carefully. When in doubt, consult your veterinarian before purchasing and using any tick-control products.

Demodectic Mange

Would you be surprised to learn that your Boston Terrier has mites? Not just a case of mites, but mites that spend their entire lives in his hair follicles and skin glands? Demodectic mange is a skin disease caused by a tiny alligator-like mite called a *Demodex canis* mite. In small numbers, these mites are typically present on your dog's skin, and in most cases they do not usually cause problems.

The development of demodicosis is complex and not completely understood, but here's what experts *do* know: the mites are passed from a mother to a puppy in the first week or so of life. Demodectic mange is not an inherited condition, but there appears to be a correlation between a puppy's ineffective or sensitive immune system, which may have a genetic component, and the mange itself. There are also two forms of the disease: localized and generalized. Localized is the most common and occurs in dogs usually under one year of age. Lesions are usually associated with some hair loss because the mites prefer to live in the hair follicles. Lesions can appear as crusty, red skin, and can occasionally a have a greasy or moist appearance. Most of these lesions are confined to the muzzle, eyes, and other areas around the head and will usually clear up as the puppy grows and develops his own immunity.

Generalized demodicosis is a more severe version and characterized by lesions and areas of hair loss over the entire body, including the head, neck, stomach, legs, and feet, with lesions commonly aggravated by secondary bacterial infections. In severe cases, dogs can become quite ill, becoming lethargic and feverish, with an attendant loss of appetite.

Demodectic mange is identified by clinical diagnosis of

lesions and skin scrapings to confirm the presence of mites. All dogs have mites, so the visual identification of lesions is an equally important part of the diagnosis. Treatment for localized cases usually involves shampoos, dips, and topical ointments or creams. Generalized cases require a more aggressive approach including dips, anti-parasitic drugs, and antibiotics to treat inflamed and infected lesions.

PROBLEMS SPECIFIC TO THE BRACHYCEPHALIC DOG

The Boston Terrier's flat face and short muzzle are part of the dog's complete package, just like his dapper black-and-white coat. Like his markings, his face is part of what distinguishes the Boston Terrier from other breeds, and helps to give the breed its unique and charming appeal. Unfortunately, what distinguishes the breed can also be a source of frustration for owners and present life-threatening medical conditions for the dogs.

Their smaller, compressed muzzles classify Boston Terriers as a brachycephalic breed.

Brachycephalic dogs, like the Boston Terrier, have the anatomical components of a regular-sized muzzle but in a much smaller, compressed space. Because of their anatomy, nearly all brachycephalic dogs have some degree of increased work associated with breathing. Simply put, they have a harder time breathing than non-brachycephalic dogs. The Boston Terrier, for instance, can have noisy mouth breathing, foamy nostrils, exercise and heat intolerance, coughing, and regurgitation of foamy saliva. These conditions can range from mild to severe. As a result of the upper airway problems, Boston Terriers are prone to overheating, and great care must be taken to prevent heatstroke.

The problems associated with brachycephalic dogs are collectively known as brachycephalic airway obstruction syndrome (BAOS), or brachycephalic syndrome, for short, and include:

- Stenotic Nares: malformed nostrils with narrow openings that restrict the amount of air a Boston can inhale through his nose. As a result, many dogs compensate by breathing through their mouths. Hence, the breed's tendency to mouth breath, and its sometimes noisy breathing. Diagnosis is made by visual examination. Surgery to open the nares is a possible option.

- Elongated Soft Palate: a condition where the palate (the flesh on the roof of the mouth) extends into the back of the throat. If too long, the soft palate hangs down into the airway just in front of the windpipe, obstructing normal airflow. Diagnosis is made by visual examination and may require sedation or anesthesia. Surgery to remove the excess tissue and widen the opening of the nares to allow for more normal respiration is a possible option.

- Everted Laryngeal Saccules are small bags or sacks of tissue that normally sit in front of the vocal cords. Problems arise when there is a decreased pressure in the upper airways and the saccules are literally pulled in front of the trachea (windpipe) and block the flow of air.

Additionally, some brachycephalic breeds are prone to tracheal collapse—a condition in which the cartilage of the trachea degenerates over time and eventually loses its ability to maintain its shape. As a result, the trachea becomes prone to collapsing during respiration.

Experts believe there is a congenital component in the makeup of the trachea. Symptoms include a harsh cough and coughing fits that become worse over time. A definitive diagnosis may require x-rays.

BREEDING BOSTON TERRIERS

The importance of leaving the breeding of Boston Terriers to the experts cannot be stressed enough. Breeding dogs should never be taken lightly, and it is significantly more complicated than merely putting a male and female together and waiting 62 days to see what pops out.

The average litter for a Boston Terrier is three puppies, but so many things can wrong.

Boston Terriers are prone to a condition called *dystocia*, which means they may have difficulty during labor and delivery. The primary stumbling block is the size of a Boston's head, which is difficult, if not impossible, to deliver naturally. Generally, the dam's pelvic bone and muscular structure will separate sufficiently to allow the passage of a puppy. However, with brachycephalic breeds that tend to have large heads and big shoulders, there is not sufficient separation to allow the head to pass through the birth canal. Therefore, nearly all Boston puppies are delivered via Cesarean surgery.

Don't be fooled into thinking your Boston Terrier will be different. Cesarean surgery is necessary if you hope to save any or all of the puppies, and these types of surgeries are not cheap. Just as important, a female that has been administered an anesthetic for delivery is not herself for a day or two after the surgery. Therefore, you must make provisions for caring for the puppies until she has completely recovered. If you try to place the puppies with her before she is fully recovered, she might accidentally hurt them.

THE SENIOR BOSTON

Boston Terriers are considered "seniors" anywhere from age seven and older. You're the best judge of when to make this call for your dog. You'll notice when he begins to slow down, isn't as interested in long walks around the neighborhood, sleeps more, seems to be getting gray around the muzzle, etc. Your veterinarian may also notice signs that indicate it's time to consider these your dog's golden years.

The breeding of Boston Terriers should be done only to preserve or advance the breed, and only after careful and thorough consideration is given to the selection of the sire and dam. Additionally, a significant amount of time and energy must go into the care and management of the pregnant female if the process is to go smoothly.

Many say that this is the best time of a dog's life. Older dogs have learned to live with their families: they know the routine, they know what to expect. Being less active themselves means you don't need to keep them as active—they're even more interested in curling up in your lap than before!

Old age has its requirements, though, just as puppyhood did. You will need to assess your dog's overall health and determine what you'll need to do to maintain it at its peak. This may mean changing his diet to one specially formulated for seniors. It may mean supplementing his food with certain vitamins, minerals, or herbs for improved skin condition or healthier joints. It may mean your dog needs to wear a sweater in cool weather and a coat when it's cold.

Mind how you interact with your senior citizen. His eyesight or hearing may be failing before it's readily apparent; be sure he hears and sees you when asking him to do things so you don't get upset with him. His bladder control may weaken, leading to accidents in the house. These are probably as upsetting to him as to you; have patience—remember, your friend won't live forever. Treasure him while you can!

SAYING GOODBYE

One of the cruelties of having animal friends is that they often die before we do, and no matter how prepared for their loss you think you may be, each is painful, and each is unique. It is your responsibility to care for your Boston the best you can when it's his time, just as you did through the rest of his life. You can make the decision of when to end his suffering, and you should if it's necessary. Hopefully it won't be a decision you need to make because of an emergency, and you'll have some time to prepare for it.

Call your veterinarian and let him or her know that you think it's time. Perhaps you'll want a final opinion. Some veterinarians make house calls to put dogs to sleep; it's worth finding out. Think about what you want to do with your dog's body once he's gone, and prepare for that. Believe it or not, it will help you later.

When the moment of truth arrives, surround your friend with his favorite things—a favorite cozy blanket, a select toy. Let everyone in the family say goodbye, if possible, including other pets. Play soothing music at your home or in the car, and try to think happy thoughts for your dog. If you're evidently very upset, he will be, too. Give him a sense of peace he deserves by projecting the sacredness of this time, not your fear. You can deal with that—and the grief—later.

When the vet comes to your home, or when you're at his office, stay with your friend. The vet will explain the procedure for giving the shot and what your dog will experience. Talk to your dog in a soothing voice. Let him know how much you love him and what your favorite times were together. Sing to him if you want. Help him pass peacefully to the other side. Take as much time as you need with him after he's passed.

After you've taken care of your dog, take care of yourself. Many people say losing a canine companion is even worse than losing a person. Dogs understand us intimately and love us unconditionally. Their loss is life-changing.

Allow yourself to grieve. Talk to people who understand, and ignore people who don't. You may want to set aside a special place in your home to put your friend's collar, toy, or other belongings where you can meditate on his memory and remember the special times you shared. These are what make sharing life with a dog so special, and why it's all worth it.

Cater to your Boston—she's earned it!

Health of Your Boston Terrier

RESOURCES

Organizations
American Kennel Club (AKC)
5580 Centerview Drive
Raleigh, NC 27606
Telephone: (919) 233-9767
Fax: (919) 233-3627
E-mail: info@akc.org
www.akc.org

Association of Pet Dog Trainers (APDT)
150 Executive Center Drive Box 35
Greenville, SC 29615
Telephone: (800) PET-DOGS
Fax: (864) 331-0767
www.apdt.com

Canadian Kennel Club (CKC)
89 Skyway Avenue, Suite 100
Etobicoke, Ontario M9W 6R4
Telephone: (416) 675-5511
Fax: (416) 675-6506
E-mail: information@ckc.ca
www.ckc.ca

Delta Society
875 124th Ave NE, suite 101
Bellevue, WA 98005
Telephone: (425) 226-7357
Fax: (425) 235-1076
E-mail: info@deltasociety.org
www.deltasociety.org

Boston Terrier Club of America
Joyce Fletcher, Corresponding Secretary
3878 Banks Rd.
Cincinnati, OH 45245
www.bostonterrierclubofamerica.org

Boston Terrier Club (UK)
Telephone: 0171 352 2436

The Boston Terrier Club of Canada
Mrs. Karen Papsen, Secretary
Telephone: 604-599-6992
www.bostonterrierclubofcanada.com

The Kennel Club (UK)
1 Clarges Street
London
W1J 8AB
Telephone: 0870 606 6750
Fax: 0207 518 1058
www.the-kennel-club.org.uk

United Kennel Club (UKC)
100 E. Kilgore Road
Kalamazoo, MI 49002-5584
Telephone: (269) 343-9020
Fax: (269) 343-7037
E-mail: pbickell@ukcdogs.com
www.ukcdogs.com

Animal Welfare Groups and Rescue Organizations
American Humane Association (AHA)
63 Inverness Drive East
Englewood, CO 80112
Telephone: (303) 792-9900
Fax: 792-5333
www.americanhumane.org

American Society for the Prevention of Cruelty to Animals (ASPCA)
424 E. 92nd Street
New York, NY 10128-6804
Telephone: (212) 876-7700
www.aspca.org

Boston Terrier National Rescue
Susan Hunter, Rescue Coordinator
btcaresq@bthaven.org
www.bostonterrierclubofamerica.org/rescue

Royal Society for the Prevention of Cruelty
to Animals (RSPCA)
Telephone: 0870 3335 999
Fax: 0870 7530 284
www.rspca.org.uk

The Humane Society of the United States
(HSUS)
2100 L Street, NW
Washington DC 20037
Telephone: (202) 452-1100
www.hsus.org

World Animal Net (USA)
19 Chestnut Square
Boston, MA 02130
Telephone: (617) 524-3670
E-mail: info@worldanimal.net
www.worldanimal.net

Emergency Phone Numbers

ASPCA ANIMAL POISON CONTROL
CENTER
(888) 426-4435
*A $50 consultation fee may be applied to
your credit card.*

National Dog Registry (NDR)
Telephone: (800) 637-3647
E-mail: info@natldogregistry.com
www.natldogregistry.com

Veterinary Resources

American Academy of Veterinary
Acupuncture (AAVA)
66 Morris Avenue, Suite 2A
Springfield, NJ 07081
Telephone: (973) 379-1100
E-mail: office@aava.org
www.aava.org

American Animal Hospital Association
(AAHA)
P.O. Box 150899
Denver, CO 80215-0899
Telephone: (303) 986-2800
Fax: (303) 986-1700
E-mail: info@aahanet.org
www.aahanet.org

American College of Veterinary
Ophthalmologists (ACVO)
P.O. Box 1311
Mediridan, Idaho 83680
Telephone: (208) 466-7624
E-mail: office@acvo.org
www.acvo.com

American Veterinary Chiropractic
Association (AVCA)
442154 E 140 Road
Bluejacket, OK 74333
Telephone: (918) 784-2231
E-mail: amvetchiro@aol.com
www.animalchiropractic.org

American Veterinary Medical Association
(AVMA)
1931 North Meacham Road, Suite 100
Schaumburg, IL 60173
Telephone: (847) 925-8070
Fax: (847) 925-1329
E-mail: avmainfo@avma.org
www.avma.org

INDEX

accidents during housetraining, 117, 118
adult dogs
adoption of, 31-32
feeding and nutritional requirements of, 67
agility competition, 138-139
AKC Family Dog, 10
AKC Gazette, 10
American Bull Terriers, 7
American Kennel Club (AKC), 8-10
Canine Good Citizen program and, 9-10, 133-134
conformation events in, 142-143
registration process with, 38-40
amino acids, 59
anal glands, 88
annual checkups in, 152
apartment life and Boston Terrier, 25
appearance, general, 14
assistance, service, therapy dogs, 146-147
Atkinson's Toby, 6
atopic dermatitis, 154-155

babesiosis, 175
bad breath (halitosis), 92
barking, 125-127
Barnard, J.P., 6
Barnard's Tom, 6
bathing, 88-89, **88**
beds and bedding, 46
begging behaviors, 75-76
bill of sale, 41-43
boarding your dog, 51-52
bones in diet, 61
Borrelia burgdorferi. See Lyme disease, 163
Boston Terrier Club of America (BTCA), 8-9, 11, 36
brachycephalic airway obstruction syndrome (BAOS), 178

brachycephalic dogs, health problems of, 177-179
Brainstem Auditory Evoked Response (BAER) tests, 40, 156
breathing, brachycephalic airway obstruction syndrome (BAOS) in, 178
breeder screening, 31, 34-36
breeding you Boston Terrier, 179
Brindle Beauty, 10
brindle color, 20
Brindle Mike, 9
brushing your Boston Terrier, 80-82
brushing your dog's teeth, 90-92, **91**
bull baiting, 6
Bull Terrier, 7
Bulldog and Boston Terrier, 6-7
Bulldog Club of America, 8
Burnett's Gyp or Kate, 6

Canadian Kennel Club (CKC), 10, 143
Canine Eye Registration Foundation (CERF), 40
canine freestyle competition, 146
Canine Freestyle Federation Inc. (CFF), 146
Canine Good Citizen program, 9-10, 133-134
carbohydrates in diet, 58-59
cataracts, 154, 155
Champion Tracker (CT), 140
characteristics of the Boston Terrier, 13-29. *See also* standards of judging, 13
chew toys, 93, 130-131
chewing, 50-51, 128-131
children and Boston Terrier, 26-27
chondroitin, 70
city life and Boston Terrier, 25
coat and skin, 20. *See also* grooming
atopic dermatitis in, 154-155
flea allergy dermatitis (FAD) in, 174
itchy skin in, 173
mange in, 176-177

coccidia, 165-166

cold weather precautions, 25, 144

collars, 46-47

color and markings, 14, 20

Come command, 107-109

not coming when called as, 127-128

Companion Dog (CD) class, 135

Companion Dog Excellent (CDX) class, 135

conformation events (dog shows),141-143

Conn, Annette, 98

contracts. *See* bill of sale

correcting your Boston Terrier, 122-125

crate training, 109-113

crates, 44-45

cropping ears, 18

daycare for dogs, 51, 52-53

deafness, 155-157

dehydrated fresh foods, 65

demodectic mange, 176-177

dental care, 89-93

bad breath (halitosis) and, 92

chew toys for, 93

teething and, 129-131. *See also* chewing

digging, 127

disciplining and correction, 122-125

distemper, 161

Dixie, 9

dog food, 61-65. *See also* feeding

doggie daycare, 51, 52-53

Down command, 101-102, 103

Down-Stay command, 105

dry food or kibble, 63-64

Dudley nose, 18

ears, 18

Brainstem Auditory Evoked Response (BAER)
tests, 40, 156

care and cleaning of, 86-87, **86**

cropping of, 18

deafness in, 155-157

infections in, 87

ehrlichiosis, 175

elderly dogs, 67-69, 179-181

end of life issues in, 180-181

feeding and nutritional requirements of, 67-69

health and medical care for, 179-181

life expectancy of, 67-68

emergency medical care, 150

end of life issues, 180-181

England and the Boston Terrier, 10

English Bull Terrier, 7

English Bulldog, 8

English Terrier, 5

Escherichia coli, 57

exercise pens, 45-46

exercise requirements, 25, 27-28, 144

heatstroke, heat exhaustion, heat prostration,
159-160

expression, 17

eyes, 17-18

Canine Eye Registration Foundation (CERF) for,
40

care and cleaning of, 87

cataracts in, 154, 155

fats in diet, 60

feeding, 55-77

adult dogs and, special requirements of, 67

begging behaviors and, 75-76

bones in, 61

carbohydrates in, 58-59

commercial dog food in, 61-65

dehydrated fresh foods in, 65

dishes for, 49

dry food or kibble in, 63-64

elderly dogs and, special requirements of, 67-69

fats in, 60

forms and formulations for, 62-65

good table manners and, 76-77

homecooked meals in, 60-61

minerals in, 57-58

nutraceuticals in, 69-71

nutritional needs vary with age in, 55-56

obesity and, 71-76

poisonous or toxic food items and, 73

premium vs. low-cost dog foods in, 62

prescription type, 62

proteins in, 59

puppies and, special requirements of, 65-67

raw foods in, 61

semi-moist foods in , 64-65
supplements for, 69
table scraps in, 73-74
treats in, 74
vitamins in, 58
water requirements in, 56-57
feet, 19
excess hair between pads and, 86
nail trimming in, 82-85, **83**
flea allergy dermatitis (FAD), 174
flea control, 172-174
flyball competition, 145-146
food dishes, 49
formal obedience competitions, 134-137
formal training, 98
French Bulldog, 7

gait, 19-20
general appearance, 14
Gentle command, 76-77
Giardia, 57, 164-165
glucosamine, 70
grooming, 79-93

Hagerty King, 7
head collars, 46
head, 16-17
health and medical care, 13, 149-181
anal glands and, 88
annual checkups in, 152
atopic dermatitis in, 154-155
babesiosis in, 175
bad breath (halitosis) in, 92
brachycephalic airway obstruction syndrome
    (BAOS) in, 178
brachycephalic dogs and, 177-179
breeding and, 179
cataracts in, 154, 155
coccidia in, 165-166
deafness in, 155-157
dental care in, 89-93
distemper in, 161
ear infections in, 87
ehrlichiosis in, 175
elderly dogs and, 179-181

emergency medical care in, 150
end of life issues in, 180-181
flea allergy dermatitis (FAD) in, 174
flea control in, 172-174
Giardia in, 164-165
heartworms in, 170-171
heatstroke, heat exhaustion, heat prostration and,
    159-160
hepatitis in, 162
hookworms in, 168-169
itchy skin in, 173
kennel cough in, 163
laryngeal saccule eversion in, 178
leptospirosis in, 162
Lyme disease in, 163-164, 175
mange and mites in, 176-177
obesity and, 71-76
parvovirus in, 162-163
patellar luxation in, 157-159
physical exams in, 152
preventive care and checkups in, 151-152
protozoal intestinal infections and, 164-166
rabies in, 163
record keeping for, 40-41
Rocky mountain spotted fever in, 175
roundworms in, 167-168
showing your dog and, 137
soft palate abnormalities in, 178
spaying and neutering in, 33-34
stenotic nares in, 178
tapeworms in, 169
Texas fever in, 175
tick control in, 174-176
tracheal collapse in, 178
tularemia in, 175
vaccinations in, 152-153
veterinarian selection for, 149-150
whipworms in, 170
worms and worming in, 166-171
health records for puppies, 40-41
hearing, Brainstem Auditory Evoked Response
    (BAER) tests, 40, 156
heartworms, 170-171
heat, in females, 33
heatstroke, heat exhaustion, heat prostration,

159-160
Hector, 9
hepatitis, 162
hiking with your dog, 144
history of Boston Terrier, 5-11
homecooked meals, 60-61
hookworms, 168-169
Hooper, Robert C., 5, 8
Hooper's Judge, 5, 6
hot weather precautions, 25, 46, 144
heatstroke, heat exhaustion, heat prostration and, 159-160
housetraining, 112-118
paper training in, 117-118

identification tags, 48, 49
Indefinite Listing Privilege (ILP), 37
informal training, 98
It's a Dog's Life, 98
itchy skin, 173

jogging with your dog, 144
joints, patellar luxation in, 157-159

Kennel Club (UK), 10
kennel clubs, 8-11
kennel cough, 163
Kennel Gazette, 10

laryngeal saccule eversion, 178
leashes, 47-48
legs, patellar luxation in, 157-159
leptospirosis, 57, 162
lifespan of Boston Terrier, 67-68
Lyme disease, 163-164, 175

majors, in conformation events, 142
male vs. female, 32-33
    judging standards for, 16
mange, 176-177
marking territory, 33
Meanwell, Peter, 139
methylsulfonylmethane (MSM), 70
microchip identification, 50
minerals, 57-58
minors, in conformation events, 142

mites, 176-177
modern-day breeding, 7-8
motivating behavior, 97-98
muzzle, 18

nail trimming , 82-85, **83**
naming the breed, 7-8
naming your puppy, 37-38
neck, 19-20
New England Kennel Club, 9
nose, 18
Dudley type, 18
not coming when called, 127-128
Novice obedience class, 135
nutraceuticals, 69-71
Nylabone, 44, 50, 93, 131

O'Brien, William, 5
Obedience Trial Champion (OTCH), 136-137
obesity , 71-76
Open obedience class, 135-136
Orthopedic Foundation for Animals (OFA), 40

paper training/housetraining in, 117-118
parvovirus, 162-163
patellar luxation, 157-159
pedigrees, 37-38
personality. See temperament and personality
pet sitters, 51, 52
pet vs. show quality dogs, 31-32
Philadelphia Dog Show, 9
physical exams in, 152
play, 27
training and, 98
poisonous or toxic food items, 73
pop and jerk training, 96
premium vs. low-cost dog foods, 62
preparing for your Boston Terrier, 31-53
prescription type diets, 62
problem behavior, 125-130
barking as , 125-127
begging, 75-76
chewing as, 128-131
digging as, 127
not coming when called as, 127-128
shaker cans in, 126-127

proteins in diet, 59
protozoal intestinal infections, 164-166
Punch, 9
puppies, 31-44
adult dogs vs., 31-32
bill of sale with, 41-43
breeder screening for, 31, 34-36
crate training and, 109-113
feeding and nutritional requirements of, 65-67
grooming and, 80
health records of, 40-41
housetraining of, 112-118
male vs. female, 32-33
naming of, 37-38
pedigrees and registration in, 37-40
puppy-proofing your home for, 43-44
rescue organizations as source for, 36-37
safety precautions for, 43-44
show vs. pet quality dogs, 31-32
socialization in, 120-122
spaying and neutering in, 33-34
training of, 96, 99-100
vaccinations for, 41, 153
puppy-proofing your home, 43-44

rabies, 163
rally obedience competitions, 137-138
raw foods diet, 61
registration process, 37-40
rescue organizations, 36-37
rewards in training, 97-98
Rocky mountain spotted fever, 175
Round Headed Bull and Terrier, 7, 8
roundworms, 167-168

safety , 43-44
seal color, 20
semi-moist foods, 64-65
service, therapy dogs, 146-147
shaker cans, 126-127
show vs. pet quality dogs, 31-32
showing your Boston Terrier, 9-10, 133-147
agility competition in, 138-139
canine freestyle competition in, 146
Companion Dog (CD) class in, 135
Companion Dog Excellent (CDX) class in, 135
conformation events (dog shows) in, 141-143
flyball competition in, 145-146
formal obedience in, 134-137
Novice obedience class in, 135
Obedience Trial Champion (OTCH) in, 136-137
Open obedience class in, 135-136
rally obedience competitions and, 137-138
tracking competition in, 139-141
Utility obedience class/Utility Dog (UD) in, 136
veterinary checkup before, 137
Sit and Accept Praise command , 105-106
Sit command, 100-101, **101**, 102
Sit-Stay command, 103-104, **104**
size, proportion, substance, 15-16
skin. *See* coat and skin
Smith, H., 10
socialization, 120-122
soft palate abnormalities, 178
spaying and neutering in, 33-34
Spider, 9
Staffordshire Terrier, 6
Stand command, 106-107, **106**
Stay command, 103-105
stenotic nares, 178
supplements to diet, 69
supplies, 44-46
swimming, 144-145

table manners, 76-77
table scraps in diet, 73-74
tail, 6, 7, 19
tapeworms,, 169
teeth. *See* dental care
temperament and personality, 7, 20-25
Texas fever, 175
therapy dogs, 146-147
tick control, 174-176
Lyme disease and, 163-164
Tobin's Kate, 6
topline and body, 19-20
Topsy, 9
toys, 50-51
tracheal collapse, 178
tracking competition, 139-141
Tracking Dog (TD), 140
Tracking Dog Excellent (TDX), 140

trainers, professional, 99-100

training, 95-131

advanced, 133-147. *See also* showing your Boston
  Terrier

age to begin, 96

anal glands and, 88

assistance, service, therapy dogs and, 146-147

basic type, 100-108

bathing in, 88-89, **88**

brushing in, 80-82

Canine Good Citizen program and, 133-134

Come command in, 107-109

crate training in, 109-113

dental care in, 89-93

disciplining and correction in, 122-125

Down command in, 101-102, 103

Down-Stay command in, 105

ear care and cleaning in, 86-87, **86**

eye care and cleaning in, 87

formal obedience in, 134-137

formal vs. informal, 98

fun and play in, 98

Gentle command in, 76-77

good table manners and, 76-77

housetraining and, 112-118

nail trimming in, 82-85, **83**

paper training/housetraining in, 117-118

pop and jerk type, 96

problem behavior and. *See* problem behavior

rally obedience competitions and, 137-138

rewards and motivation in, 97-98

shaker cans in, 126-127

Sit and Accept Praise command in, 105-106

Sit command in, 100-101, **101**, 102

Sit-Stay command in, 103-104, **104**

socialization in, 120-122

Stand command in, 106-107, **106**

Stay command in, 103-105

tracking competition in, 139-141

trainers for, 99-100

types of, 95-97

traveling with your Boston Terrier, 53

treats, 74

tularemia, 175

United Kennel Club, 11

urination as territory marking, 33

Utility obedience class/Utility Dog (UD), 136

vaccinations, 41, 152-153

Variable Surface Tracker (VST), 140-141

Varley, John, 139

veterinarian care, 149-150. *See also* health and
  medical care

vitamins, 58

walking your dog, 144

water requirements, 56-57

weight, 15-16

Well's Eph, 6

Westminster Kennel Club, 143

whipworms, 170

World Canine Freestyle Organization Inc.
  (WCFO), 146

worms and worming, 166-171

Acknowledgements

A special thanks to my husband, Paul, whose love and encouragement have been the constant in my life, enabling me the opportunity to write and train dogs every day.

Special thanks to Leonard Myers and Patricia Stone for their time, patience, and historical research; Dr. Wendy Wallace, DVM, for her expertise, proof reading, and for unselfishly lending a helping hand; Colin Sealy at England's prestigious Kennel Club for his research; and all of the interesting and remarkable BTCA members I have had the good fortune to speak with along the way. There have been so many that to mention them all would fill an entire book! To Bobbie Anderson for her training insight and words of wisdom, and to Heather Russell-Revesz at TFH Publications, Inc., for her guidance.

Photo Credits

Photos courtesy of Isabelle Francais

Nylabone® Cares.

Dogs of all ages, breeds, and sizes have enjoyed our world-famous chew bones for over 50 years. For the safest, healthiest, and happiest lifetime your dog can possibly have, choose from a variety of Nylabone® Pet Products!

Toys   Treats   Chews   Crates   Grooming

Available at retailers everywhere. Visit us online at www.nylabone.com